THE TRUTH ABOUT MEN

ALSO BY IAN K. SMITH, M.D.

Eat

Happy

The 4 Day Diet

Extreme Fat Smash Diet

The Fat Smash Diet

The Take-Control Diet

Dr. Ian Smith's Guide to Medical Websites

The Blackbird Papers: A Novel

THE TRUTH ABOUT MEN

THE SECRET SIDE OF THE OPPOSITE SEX

Ian K. Smith, M.D.

ST. MARTIN'S PRESS

NEW YORK

Book design by Ellen Cipriano

ISBN 978-1-250-00427-7

To Tristé . . . Without Limits . . . Eternally

CONTENTS

ACKNOWLEDGMENTS

I want to thank all of my female friends, who have been wonderful and generous in sharing the highs and lows and embarrassments of their relationships and trusting me enough to request my advice in these delicate matters. Thanks also to my guy friends, who have given me enough stories and opinions to not only laugh for the rest of my life, but to fill up an entire library of books.

INTRODUCTION

The final spark that got me to sit down and finally write this book happened one afternoon in the great city of New York. I was sitting in a room filled with more than three hundred women who were supposed to be attending a seminar on how they could get "their health groove back." Having written several health books and sat on many health panels in the past, I was interested in hearing what the panelists were going to say to this group of well-educated, well-heeled women who enjoyed many advantages that others don't—serious, accomplished women who were influential in their workplaces as well as in their homes and community organizations.

I sat there—one of only two men in the room—and listened. The topic of the seminar was important, as women are certainly the gatekeepers of the family's health, and the panelists started talking about the health struggles that women endure in this role. They spoke of the need to put their health first and not always worry about others, neglecting themselves. Then the topic of men came up and the tension in the room spiked dramatically. The lightning-rod issue of how to find the right man and keep him was now center stage, and it transformed these rather sedate and dignified women into an angry pack of firebrands. They reacted as if they were at a pep rally. I was happy to be sitting close to the exit, where I was largely ignored and could make a hasty escape if necessary.

What really got my attention, however, was the seemingly endless commentary from Panelist #1. While I was in a rather relaxed mood, all things considered, she really started to wear on my nerves. She was Ms. Know-It-All: *Girlfriends, let me tell you what you need to do to get that man. Girlfriends, let me tell you about the power you have and don't even know. Girlfriends, men are completely afraid of commitment.* On and on she went as if she were omniscient and everyone else in the room merely students in desperate need of her wisdom to save them from burning in relationship hell. What pissed me off the most was not the topic, not even the male-bashing that was going on, as some of it was well deserved. Over the years I had found myself many times counseling my own female friends about their "men issues." No, what pissed me off was that this know-it-all didn't know very much at all. She sounded good, spoke well, and was quite attractive in her expensively tailored suit and Louboutin heels, but almost everything out of her mouth was utter nonsense.

I wanted to stand up and tell these women, who were so badly looking for answers, the *real reasons* a man wants a woman to pick up the restaurant tab every once in a while. I wanted to tell them the *real reasons* a man doesn't want them to have a key to his apartment, or why he's not so charged up to meet their family, even after a couple of months of dating. I had an electric urge to stand up right there in that sea of charged estrogen and give them the pure, unadulterated truth, the truth that I knew would be painful to some and considered disrespectful by others, but would be the truth nonetheless. At the very least it would be much more informative, accurate, and helpful than the ridiculous meanderings of Panelist #1.

But instead of standing up, I turned over the conference program I had found underneath my seat and started taking notes on the back. I wrote furiously over the next forty-five minutes, outlining some of the major misperceptions that were getting in the way of being able to understand men better. I captured the advice dispensed by the panelists and the questions—excellent questions in fact—from the audience. I made up my mind right then and there that, even if my fellow XY compatriots might brand me a traitor, I was going to tell the honest and painful truth to women. I was going to pull back the curtains that hide a man's mind and bare the inner workings of how we think and why we think the way we do. Panelist #1 would be my writing muse, and the wonderful and intelligent women who sat and listened to her every word would now be *my* audience as I would let women know what men *want* them to know but *won't* tell them.

THE TRUTH ABOUT MEN

THE FIRST

THE SUBTLE ART OF HOOKING US

There's a big misperception that men never want to be in committed relationships if we can help it, and that we prefer to have the freedom to date a harem of women. Not so. We want to be in a committed relationship, but it has to be with the right woman at the right time.

LET'S START WITH a simple truth. Men don't want to feel like they're being hooked, especially in the beginning of a relationship. This has something to do with our innate desire for freedom and our need to feel like we're in control. Not to say that we're not open to the idea of settling down and being satisfied in a monogamous relationship with you, but the second we detect that these are your intentions, we either stop returning your phone calls or start figuring out ways to escape without hurting your feelings. Understanding the basics of how we think in this situation will go a long way toward producing the results that you desire. So don't judge what follows as being politically incorrect or rude. Be warned that this is not about what's right or wrong, respectful or disrespectful. This book is about one thing—the raw truth.

The Physical Matters—Period

Forget all those relationship expert columns that tell you it's most important to your man that he first see what's in your heart. Bullshit. It's most important to see what's inside your clothes. Now, before you scream, "Piiiiiiiiiiiiiiiiig!" listen carefully. I'm not saying that we need to get into your pants right away in order to enjoy your company. But I am saying that men definitely need to know that you have the goods and that you take care of yourself. To put it bluntly, a guy's first interest in a woman has nothing to do with the handbag she's carrying or that she graduated from an Ivy League school. **What your (potential) man wants you to know but won't tell you is that his initial attraction is all about your appearance and physical being, which sends a flood of highly charged testosterone racing through his veins.** Yes, the physical is first, and we're not saying we won't eventually fall in love with your intelligence, kindness, and humor. These extremely important attributes are the ones that will ultimately be critical in helping you hook us. But in the beginning the number-one attribute is what you look like and how well you take care of yourself.

The glossy magazines that litter the newsstands do a real disservice to you all by defining beauty in such a narrow way. A quick flip through the pages and it's boringly obvious that most of the models and celebrities featured in these magazines are really a variation on the same theme. The truth for us men, however, is that beauty is diverse and idiosyncratic. (Great news for you.) Some of us want the well-endowed woman, while others are repulsed by the surgically enhanced. Some of us want tall and slim, while others want short and curvaceous. Some of us want you to have some "junk in the trunk," while others want it small and tight. There really is some truth to the saying, "There's a lid for every pot." The challenge for most women, however, is finding that fit.

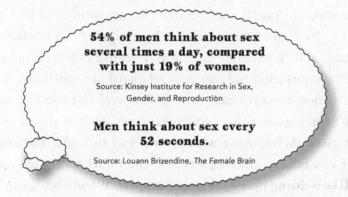

54% of men think about sex several times a day, compared with just 19% of women.

Source: Kinsey Institute for Research in Sex, Gender, and Reproduction

Men think about sex every 52 seconds.

Source: Louann Brizendine, *The Female Brain*

For some the search can be long and difficult, and for others it can be quick and easy. A lot of variables go into the length, ease, and success of that search, but the one thing that will boost your efforts is how well you present yourself. It's imperative, especially early on, that you look your best every time we see you, at least for the first few months of the relationship. This is not men being vain or superficial. Unless your father is Bill Gates, how you look is the strongest magnet you possess. Your hair must be done, your nails neatly painted, and your clothes should highlight your assets and hide your liabilities. Loose sweats, uncombed hair pulled back under a baseball cap, and rundown Ugg boots are fine once the relationship is in high gear, but definitely a turn-off when at the beginning. In our minds, if you are not making the effort to look your best when we barely know each other, we dread the thought of what you'll look like a couple of months into the relationship.

The Unnecessary Pressure of Titles

Let the royals care about titles. One of the biggest mistakes you can make during the early hook is to suggest or even hint that things have started to formalize by assigning the labels "girl-friend" and "boyfriend." Even if you feel like things are going in the right direction and that your relationship is getting more se-rious, there's an extremely wide gulf between just being someone you're dating and someone who has been officially proclaimed a boyfriend. **What your man wants you to know but won't tell you is that affixing titles to the relationship too early is like holding up a cross to a vampire**. We will often run fast and hard when we feel like we're being boxed into something we don't want or is too premature.

So, what's the resolution for you if calling him your boy-friend and yourself his girlfriend means a lot to you? The first option is simply to wait until you're absolutely sure he feels the same way about making it official. Often we give subtle signs to indicate we're ready. If we start talking about dating you exclu-sively, you can take that as a sign. If we introduce you to our close friends on several occasions, that's a solid sign. If we let you stay in our apartment when we're not there, that's a *really* good sign. The number-one sign that we're ready to go formal—we invite you to dinner with our mother. (Yes, it's our mother that counts for this one, not our dad.)

If you're not satisfied with waiting for our signs, or you think you might not be able to read them, here's something you might try that could get the ball rolling faster. Be advised, however, that if you don't do this with the proper amount of skill and cool, then it can dramatically backfire: When he calls you up and asks if you want to go grab something to eat or catch a movie, don't answer him right away. Take a deliberate pause, and in your most apologetic voice say something that will test him. "I'd love to, but one of my girlfriends has been trying like crazy to get me to meet one of her brother's friends, and we were supposed to all get together tonight. I don't want to go, but I feel like I owe it to her since she's been trying so hard to make this happen." What comes next is critical. You need to listen very carefully and might need to read between the lines of what he says. Here are some of his possible responses:

A. *Okay, fine. Well, have fun and call me when you want to get together again.*

B. *You're going on a blind date? What's up with that?*

C. *Oh, I didn't know it was like that. I guess I should be going out with other people, too.*

D. *If I'm not enough for you, then no biggie. It's probably best we not see each other anymore.*

E. *So you were just gonna go out on this date and not tell me?*

There's a lot you need to take in with each of these responses, and how you handle them can work in your favor in a big way.

(A) Depending on his tone, he's either jealous but doesn't want to let on, he's neutral and it's okay, or he's pissed off and doesn't want you to see how angry he is. This isn't the most optimal response, because now you have to do a little detecting to figure out what he's really feeling, whether you need to nurse his wound or accept that he really doesn't care, in which case he's probably out there dating others so he's not going to give you a hard time. Your next step is to figure out what he wanted to say but didn't. Once you figure this part out, then you can react accordingly.

(B) This response gives you a perfect opportunity to bring up whether you're officially girlfriend and boyfriend without his feeling like you're pressuring him. Say to him in your most innocent voice, "We never talked about dating exclusively, and technically I'm not even your girlfriend, so I just figured it wasn't a big deal to you." Now the title issue is on the table, and he has to address it directly since he's the one who had a problem with your going out on a date with someone else. If you get this response, you are in a great position to stick in the hook.

(C) Once again you have a prime opportunity to bring up whether or not things have gotten serious enough to go exclusive as boyfriend and girlfriend. See your response in B.

(D) His ego has definitely been bruised. He wants to tell you that you mean more to him than someone he's been casually dating, but he's having a hard time saying it. Rather than get into a back-and-forth about being more into you than you are into him, he makes the decision to just cut ties and run. Once again you have a chance to reel him in (as he has now exposed a vulnerability), but you must be strong and patient as you do so or he might slip away.

(E) Needless to say, this is a response from someone who is not exactly delighted about the current state of affairs. This response could go a couple of ways, so listen to his tone and make a judgment call. If it sounds

Men were asked what is the most important personality trait when deciding if a woman is "relationship material."

34% A sense of loyalty
23% A sense of humor
21% A sense of caring/nurturing
21% Intelligence

Source: The Great Male Survey, 2010, Askmen.com

like he's really upset and thinks that you were "cheating or being sneaky," first you need to calm him. Once this is accomplished, then you can introduce the possibility of taking the relationship to the next stage. But you must be careful. If he's really upset and becomes reactive or irrational, now is not the time to have the conversation about formalizing the relationship. However, if he appears somewhat annoyed but still reasonable, then go ahead and explain to him that you were not aware that the relationship was exclusive, especially since you weren't officially girlfriend and boyfriend, but if he wants to take the relationship to the next level, you're more than happy to go there.

Occasionally Unavailable, We Want You More

What your man wants you to know but won't tell you is that he is even more attracted to you when you're not always available to him. It's true that a guy looking for a one-night stand will only continue to converse and set you (and your girlfriends) up with drinks if he knows that at the end of the night he's going to get what he wants. That's not the guy you're looking for, so let's ignore that relatively small percentage of my brethren. But if you're looking to establish a relationship with the typical guy who's not some horn dog, you need to know that although he wants to spend time with you, he also wants to feel like you won't always be able to drop everything just because he calls you up and says, "Let's go out in an hour."

It's true, especially of us men, that what we can't have we tend to want even more. Not that we want you to be unavailable the majority of the time—that won't work, either, and we'd eventually stop calling and start looking somewhere else. While we hope you want to be with us every time we call, not being able to because you have other commitments is acceptable. The other commitments, of course, should not be dates with other men, and if they are, then don't tell us. Even if you don't have something else to do, it's still in your best interest to turn us down every once in a while. Just make sure you do it with your uniquely feminine charm, and leave the conversation on an up note. Telling us that while tonight won't work, but you want to see us really soon prevents us from personalizing the rejection, because now we will leave the conversation feeling that if you didn't have other commitments you would've hung out with us. Even though we might not get what we want, that small ego stroke will go a long way.

A significant part of hooking us early means being careful not to send the wrong message. Though you think you're making us happy by always dropping everything to be with us, it can send unintended messages. And remember, we're men. In most cases you don't want to leave us to our own devices to interpret the nuances of what you're trying to convey. In our minds, being always available to us could mean more than you simply like us a lot. We might start thinking that you don't have a life of your own and have nothing else to do but hang out with us. If, in the beginning of our relationship, you already seem quite wrapped up in us, then we worry about what's going to happen when the relationship gets more serious. Are you going to suffocate us to death?

Too available can also mean too easy. If you don't present somewhat of a challenge to us, then we lose what is often one of the most exciting aspects of a budding relationship—the thrill of the hunt. **What your man wants you to know but won't tell you is that he doesn't mind having to put in some work (but not an overwhelming amount) to win you over**. Too much work—calling you more than three times before you return the call or agree to go out on a date—is also a problem. We're not going to stick around if we feel like we're at the bottom of a steep hill trying to push a two-ton boulder to the top. Still, we enjoy challenges, so if you can throw in some twists and turns on our path to your heart, we'll be more inclined to put forth a greater effort and see things to their culmination.

THE SITUATION

You meet a guy at a friend's birthday party. You're attracted to him immediately. He's good-looking but not cocky, funny but not trying to be the life of the party. He is obviously well informed and has something smart to say about everything from politics to the recent slate of Oscar-nominated films. All the single women at the party have made their attempts, but he has politely sent them away empty-handed.

The two of you strike up a conversation, because he's interested in the gold and jade earrings that you're wearing. He says his grandmother had a similar pair that she passed down to his mother. You tell him the story of your earrings and how your grandfather bought them for your mother when he was stationed as a young serviceman in Japan. One conversation leads to another and before you know it, you're standing on a balcony overlooking the city, laughing at each other's jokes and comparing notes on the television shows you love to hate. He leaves with your phone number and e-mail address in his BlackBerry.

Three months have passed and dating him has gone extremely well. Your girlfriends think he's the catch of the year, and his friends couldn't be more welcoming. One day, at the encouragement of one of your girlfriends, you decide to join Facebook. You've resisted joining all this time because you've seen so many people get addicted to it, but she insists that it's so much fun and a great way to find and stay connected with old friends as well as make new ones. It takes you a few weeks to get comfortable in this whole social-networking arena, and you find that despite your early doubts you're actually enjoying it.

You decide to find your boyfriend's page, so you do a search. His surname is unique and you find him within seconds. You get to his page, and it's not like you're trying to be nosy or anything, but you decide to look around a little. The first thing you notice is the info section and it stops you cold. Under the section "Interested In" it says "Women." Under the section "Relationship Status" it says "Single." When you set up *your* Facebook page, you made certain to list men as your interest. In the "Relationship Status" section, *you* had indicated you were unavailable. You go to his wall and look at his photo gallery. There are 115 photos and the only one of you is in a group shot taken at a restaurant. You weren't even sitting next to him. You search his entire page and there's no mention or even an indication that the two of you are dating. You go back to his info page and can't take your eyes off the line that says he's single. He isn't acknowledging that you are dating. *So now what do you do?*

(See The Handle #1)

Mandates Will Keep You Manless

One of my best friends and I were having dinner at a very popular restaurant in the Meatpacking District of New York City. The place was crowded with hip young professionals out after work for a drink and great food. It was a classic scene—attractive women decked out in the latest designer fashions and guys with expensive oversized watches, full of bravado, sending drinks up and down the bar in an effort to catch the attention of women. A table of women sat next to us, and in this restaurant the tables were practically on top of one another, so it felt like a community dinner. Things happen the way they often happen with single, fun-seeking people, and before dessert had been served my friend scored the number of one of the really attractive women who had been full of conversation and flirtatious banter.

The following week, after they had talked a couple of times

on the phone and exchanged a few text messages, he asked her out to dinner. My friend has never suffered from lack of female attention, but I noticed that he was really excited about this date. All was set and he had lined up a reservation at one of the city's hottest restaurants. I wanted him to be successful for his sake, but admittedly there was an underlying selfishness to my rooting for him. If they hit it off there was a really good chance I would once again be in the company of her girlfriends—all of whom were attractive. I went to the gym while they went out, anxiously waiting to hear the report.

Disaster! My heart fell two feet when he recounted what happened. Yes, she looked amazing. Yes, she was successful in her career. Yes, she made great conversation. But where everything turned south was when she got on a riff about what she required from men who wanted to date her. Her list was longer than an Amtrak commuter train. It was one mandate after another. *A man must bring me fresh flowers when he picks me up at my apartment. A man must always take me out to eat before or after we go to the movies. A man must never pick up his phone if we're in the middle of a conversation. A man must always carry my drink from the bar to our table when we sit down to eat.* I was getting nauseous just listening to him. Needless to say, despite how physically attracted my friend was to her, it was their first and only date. He found himself staring up a hill that had a ninety-degree slope. Forget it. **What your man wants you to know but won't tell you is that if there're too many rules in the beginning of a relationship, he's gone.** Too complicated too soon is a strong indication to us that things will only get worse. We are well aware that the numbers are in our favor, so we'll play the odds and wait for someone who doesn't give us so much hassle.

It's completely fine for you to have certain requirements that you expect a man to meet if you're going to have a relationship. We know that you all have your list of *musts,* and you should. But you have to be careful of the length of this list or you will find yourself creating an ideal that simply doesn't exist in the real world. "He must be over six feet, have a college degree, make six figures a year, speak two languages, have washboard abs, never have been previously engaged, live on his own, like the same kind of music, be sensitive . . ." I've heard about these "must lists" from some of my female friends who were frustratingly single. There was no doubt in my mind why they couldn't hook a man. There was no chance in hell they could find a man who could meet their ridiculously long list of mandates. The first thing I told them was to either cut the list down or create an A list and a B list. The A list should be the things that were non-negotiable, while the B list should be things that they would like to have in an ideal situation but could do without and still be content. Two of my female friends took my advice and literally within three months their year-long drought ended and they were happily dating again.

The second thing to be careful about when sharing your mandates with a prospective boyfriend is timing. It's fine to reveal a couple of items from your list, but releasing them all at once in rapid fire is overwhelming. Think of it as the difference between being fired upon by a single-action six-shooter versus a machine gun. We can duck and dodge the six-shooter, but we stand no chance against a machine gun, even if the shooter's aim is bad. If your goal is to kill a potential relationship, delivering all of your mandates at once is a sure way to reach it.

The More Others Look, the More We Want You

Men want other men to want their women. It's that basic, and it's all related to male ego. I remember one of my best friends dating a stunning woman who was almost six feet tall, with an angled jaw, thick dark hair that fell generously down her back, and light blue eyes that glowed like headlights. She was so attractive that even women would stare at her in awe. Some of my friend's proudest moments were when he watched other men watch her as she walked across a crowded room or bar with those long, purposeful strides cutting a direct path to where he was sitting. Those ten or fifteen seconds that it took for her to complete her journey felt like an hour as heads swiveled, mouths opened, and eyes squinted. **What your man wants you to know but won't tell you is that he wants you even more when others want you.**

When the hottest woman in the room that every eye is following sits down and kisses us, it feels like a crate of fireworks is going off inside our body. Not only is it a quiet statement to the other guys in the room that we have our act together, but it is an absolute turn-on. I, too, had gotten lucky meeting a great woman from Chicago. Every time I watched other guys watch my date, I not only wanted her even more, but it was another affirmation that I was fortunate to have her and should do everything in my power to keep her. She didn't know this, but she was hooking me simply by others wanting her.

Being desirable, however, doesn't mean you go out and get the shortest dress, the highest heels, and a severely plunging neckline that all scream you want attention. Any guy is going to take a second look at a woman dressed like that, so it doesn't count. But there are other ways to be desirable that don't require physical beauty. You can put yourself together in a classy way that still draws the immediate attention of others, and something magical happens to the guy who walks out of the restaurant with you on his arm. Carrying yourself with confidence and elegance can go further and last longer and is always going to make us want you even more.

The Eight-Letter Word

Marriage. This word is one of the greatest land mines on your path to a stable and deepening relationship. Let's first dispense with the myths. Men *do* want to get married. Not all men are look-

Men were asked to choose the ultimate male status symbol.

36% Having a family.
26% Having a high-profile career.
21% Having a beautiful wife or girlfriend.

Source: The Great Male Survey, 2010, Askmen.com

ing to be bachelors into their eighties only to marry a relatively pubescent twenty-something-year-old. Marriage does not scare us. It's so easy to blame everything on us for not wanting to get married, but the simple truth is that we are open and excited about marriage—with the right person at the right time, of course.

What your man wants you to know but won't tell you is that early use of the word "marriage" is an instant red flag, even if you're using it in the most innocent of ways.

Men are programmed to stay as far away as possible from marriage conversations, because once we go there we know it's like opening up a floodgate with the exit blocked off. There is no way out. We are coached on this subject by our fathers and uncles and older friends. Usually they start with, "Listen, champ. Don't make the same mistake I made," and then the lesson begins. Typically they explain that it wasn't a mistake to get married, but it's the timing of their marriage that they regret, be it from getting married too early in life before they had a chance to sow their oats to wishing they had been with their wife longer so that they understood her better before tying the knot. It's when we enter into our late teens and our relationships with girls start taking on more serious consequences and overtones, we start getting counseled on the perils of rushed or ill-advised marriages.

Even if you think that we are marriage material—even if you are really excited about getting married—it is not the smartest move to broach the subject before you've been going out with someone for at least a year. Why a year? Well, there's nothing magical about it, but if your relationship has lasted at least a year, something is working and things are stable enough that a mention of the eight-letter word isn't going to freak your man out and make him run. But even then, you have to exercise caution. Rather than take the direct approach, you might make an innocent comment related to something you're reading—a celebrity getting engaged or an invitation you've received to a friend's wedding. The stealth approach almost always works better than tackling this issue head-on. Coming at it sideways won't scare your man, and he will be more inclined to participate, because it will strike him as just another casual conversation rather than a full-on, intense talk you've been waiting to spring on him at the right moment.

On the flip side, a lot of women think that they're making themselves more attractive to men by stating that they don't want to get married, or don't want children. This might not matter to a guy who's in his teens or early twenties, but for an older guy it's something that will undoubtedly backfire. You might think that making these proclamations—whether true or false—will create the appealing image in your man's mind that you're just a free spirit willing to have a good time without any need for commitment, but you're really boxing yourself into a position from which it's going to be difficult to escape. Yes, your man might lower his marriage guard and partner with you in what he thinks will be a relaxed and satisfying relationship. You even may have him hooked, but that hook is attached to a very flimsy string that can break any minute.

Men don't mind having a good time with women, but if they perceive you to be someone who doesn't have long-term potential, you've placed an automatic cap on your relationship, and we will think of and treat you in a manner consistent with someone who will not be around years down the road. If this is what you want, then you're all set. But if you really want a deeper relationship, then you are in trouble for the simple fact that his mindset and the way he views you are going to be difficult to change. You've offered him an extended version of going to Vegas or South Beach or wherever the good times roll, and that it's completely acceptable to hook up with a girl he might not see past the weekend. In a sense you now have become that weekend girl—permanently. Because you're the one who voluntarily put yourself in that box, he feels completely fine having fun with you, all the while still looking for that "right" woman, the woman who will bear his children, take long walks on the beach, and grow old with him. You might not notice any obvious signs of his pursuing another relationship, but you can be certain that his mind is open and he is quietly surveying the landscape for that special someone. And when that person flies across his radar, he's going to lock target and fire. He will leave you in a second to go collect his prize and not feel a single ounce of guilt, because you're the one who gave him the gun permit by saying that you don't see yourself getting married or having children or both. Remember, the danger of playing games in a relationship is that there's always a chance—regardless of how small or large—that you might come out on the losing side.

THE HANDLE #1

Before you ask him any questions, ask yourself the first one: Have the two of you agreed to be in an exclusive relationship? If the answer is yes, then you should definitely have concerns about his status posting. Giving him the benefit of the doubt, he might've forgotten to change the status after the two of you got together, but this is unlikely. Avid Facebookers regularly update their pages.

The other thing that should give you pause is that there are no real photos of the two of you showing you're together. The only photo out of 115 of you is in a group shot, which is another strong sign that something is amiss.

If the two of you have not agreed on an exclusive relationship or haven't discussed it, now is not the time to attack him, but you do need to have this conversation ASAP. You need to confront the issue without being confrontational. The worst thing you could do is go after him in an accusatory fashion that would immediately provoke him to defend himself or strike out verbally, and this would not be productive.

Try a softer approach. It might even be helpful to throw in a little humor:

"Can I submit my application?" you jest.

"Application for what?" he says.

"To be in a relationship with you."

"What are you talking about? We're in a relationship."

You give him that squinted-eye look with your head half-cocked. Your body language remains light and accessible.

"I was hoping you'd say that," you say. "Then you might want to update your Facebook page. It still says that you're single."

There are several ways to execute this conversation, but the bottom line is to get an honest answer from him without accusing him and getting into a shouting match. You want him to tell the truth about what he feels about your relationship but you don't want him to give you answers under duress because he's simply trying to placate you. Remember, you can attract more bees with honey than you can with vinegar.

CHEAT SHEET

WHAT YOU KNOW *NOW*

A man's initial attraction is all about your appearance and physical being that sends a lot of highly charged testosterone racing through his veins.

Affixing titles to the relationship too early is like holding up a cross to a vampire.

Men are even more attracted to you when you're not always available.

Men don't mind having to put in some work (but not an overwhelming amount) to win you over.

Too many rules in the beginning of a relationship and your man is gone.

Men want you even more when others want you.

Use of the word "marriage" is an instant red flag, even if you're using it in the most innocent way.

THE
SECOND

BE A FREAK, BUT NOT A FREAK OF THE WEEK

Certain male principles are very simple to understand if you're willing to accept them as statement of fact. It's simply who we are even if it doesn't make sense to you. Sex is not the only guiding force in our life, but it is definitely one of the most important. Harness our sexual energy and you will have the upper hand without our even knowing.

S EX IS A way to get a man, and keep a man, but also to lose a man. Yes, men want more than a beautiful woman and great sex, but let's be honest. If the sex isn't there, pretty soon he won't be there. Don't roll your eyes at this statement, but *men love sex*. It makes us do crazy things and make bad decisions. It's embedded deeply in our biological and cultural DNA, and regardless of how unemotional you think we are or how much you want us to see you for more than your sexual attributes, you're wasting your time if you think you can overtake those tiny but powerful blueprints of life that we call DNA.

Sex Is More Powerful Than an AK-47

Sex is *great*. It can be fun and relaxing and frustrating all at the same time. What most women don't understand is that sex is a powerful weapon in their arsenal that, used in the right way, can almost always get the results you want. But blatantly using sex as leverage is the absolutely wrong way to get what you want from a man. You might be able to do that a couple of times, holding back the good stuff until he relents on some point or issue you're worried about, but beware. Go to the well too often and you'll find there's no water left. In other words, that's what happens with what I call the sex-gun. Shoot it too many times and you run out of bullets or your man simply runs away from you.

Don't get me wrong. I'm not saying you have to jump in the sack the first time you meet a man or go out on an official date. In fact, if you do that, the odds are extremely stacked against having a long-lasting relationship with this man. But if you only want a physical relationship that might be short-term in nature, by all means act on your lustful desires. Women have every right to want a physical relationship as much as men do without being branded cheap or slutty. Many European women are masters at it and should be applauded for not believing in some outdated tradition that women must always want an emotional relationship along with sex.

If a man really wants to have sex with you—and it's not just a one-night-stand attempt in some dark, odorous bar with bad music playing too loudly—then he will wait a *certain* amount of time to have sex. Notice that I carefully used the word "certain." How long a time a man is willing to wait depends on the man. I've had friends wait for six months. Then I've had friends who were only willing to wait a couple of weeks. There's no carved-in-stone number for what that waiting period should be, but there is a set rule about physical contact. If you're not going to have sex right away, men want to know that you are at least willing to engage in some level of intimacy. And this doesn't mean a kiss when he drops you off at the door. Sufficient maybe a century ago, but certainly not now.

Men are willing to stick around and wait for the full meal as long as you're willing to at least serve up an appetizer—but this appetizer must be delectable and an indicator of how tasty the full meal will be when it's finally ready to be served. This might sound crazy because there are so many misperceptions about men, but believe it or not, most men *do not* want full sex on the first or even the second date. Men want a reasonable challenge. The first thing we think when you hop in bed with us too easily is, "Wow, this is awesome. For once I don't have to play all of the stupid games." But the second thing we think is, "Hmmm. If she let me have it so fast, how many other guys have had it the same way?" Too fast also makes men think that you could be prone to stepping out of a relationship and hooking up with other men while we're not watching. In other words, you could be a "loose woman." This is a perception you *never* want and one that is almost impossible to change.

I have a friend who is quite an attractive woman, very smart, funny, with a great job that easily affords her financial independence. She, however, has decided to abstain from sex until she has the wedding ring. She has her reasons and the right to put conditions on who she decides to do it with and when, but then she worries and sighs and constantly complains about how tough it is to find a man. She's frustrated and fearful that her egg count is dwindling down into the danger zone, and her parents are making not-so-subtle hints that they'd like to hold at least one grandchild before they cross over to the other side. I finally had to sit down and tell her the simple truth. If you think there are a lot of men who are willing to wait for marriage before they have sex, then you might as well be living in a cave in Bangladesh. And if you want someone who is attractive, financially secure, sensitive, and smart on top of being willing to wait for sex, you might as well go and play Powerball. You have a much better chance of hitting the Megabucks Jackpot than you do finding that "perfect, sex-subdued mate," 99.9 percent of whom are in such high demand they can have their pick on any given day. And most of your competitors are offering a lot more than you are by not holding back on the big prize, making the playing field so uneven it's almost impossible to win. With those odds, sooner or later you're going to be forced to compromise or grow old, lonely, bitter, and full of regrets. But if you decide to take this ill-advised route, at the very least you need to be willing to engage in some sexual intimacy—enough to arouse his curiosity—or he might not come back for more.

What your man wants you to know but won't tell you is that he doesn't always need to hit a home run to relieve his sexual tension or have a good time. Sometimes just a base hit will do. Despite the widespread belief that we want all or nothing, the truth is that we are okay with just fooling around as long as we know that later down the road there's more coming for us. There has to be something that satisfies our sexual curiosity and drive, because making us go home empty-handed every time is a sure way to make us stay away or stray away.

Sex is definitely a way to keep your man. Sure, he will stick around if he finds you interesting and loving and funny, but all of these things don't overpower the magnetism of sex. It's not just the volume of sex in a relationship that counts. In fact, if your sex is good and exciting, you can actually have less of it and your man will be satisfied. Some couples for various reasons are unable to have sex frequently, but because their sexual experience is so satisfying and varied, the man keeps coming back and is less likely to stray.

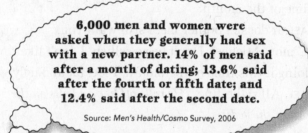

6,000 men and women were asked when they generally had sex with a new partner. 14% of men said after a month of dating; 13.6% said after the fourth or fifth date; and 12.4% said after the second date.

Source: *Men's Health/Cosmo* Survey, 2006

If men had to make a choice between variety and volume, they would choose both—of course. Your man wants you to know that he needs a minimum amount of sex. There's no magic number here. It's unique, something you need to learn from him. Don't be afraid. The easiest thing might be to ask your partner if that number exists for him and, if so, what it is. If you're too uncomfortable asking, or you feel it's too mechanical an approach, one that might lessen the spontaneity of your sex life, then figure it out on your own by observing the moods and wants of your man as you vary the number of sexual encounters.

Your Period Doesn't Stop *His* Sexual Urge

Believe it or not, one of the most optimal times to score points with your man—even better, points that are redeemable at a later time—is during your menstrual cycle. **What your man**

wants you to know but won't tell you is, even though it's that time of the month, he still has certain needs and he'd appreciate it if you could satisfy them. Follow this typical conversation between partners:

LISA: I can't, Michael. Now is not a good time. It's that time of the month.

MICHAEL: It doesn't bother me. I still want you.

LISA: C'mon, Michael. Don't be so selfish. I don't like doing it this time of the month. I feel fat and ugly.

MICHAEL: All right, fine. *(He rolls off her and sits on the side of the bed.)*

LISA: Oh, so now you can't get what you want, you're leaving.

MICHAEL: You just don't get it. *(Michael shakes his head, walks out of the bedroom, and turns on the TV in the living room.)*

This is how the conversation could've gone and both could've been satisfied.

LISA: I can't, Michael. Now is not a good time. It's that time of the month.

MICHAEL: It doesn't bother me. I still want you.

LISA: I'm happy to hear that you want me all the time, even when I have my period. But I just can't get into it. But that doesn't mean we can't have a little fun.

MICHAEL: Really?

LISA: You bet. *(Lisa proceeds to take off her shirt and bra and then helps disrobe Michael. She takes control of the situation and engages him to completion.)*

Many women don't want to have intercourse while they have their period. And as horny as men can be, most also don't want to have intercourse while you have your period. Whew! So we're on the same page. But this is where things break down. Just because you don't want to have sex and your man doesn't want to have sex, doesn't mean he still doesn't want to be pleasured. Basically, a man's libido is "menstruation-proof." Don't get me wrong. Men are empathetic and sensitive about your time of the month, but they still would like to have pleasure. Some women will scream, "That's selfish. If I can't get there, then why should he?" That is the wrong attitude to take and it will not score any points. Your man completely understands that you prefer not to go there, but he also understands that there's a lot that can be accomplished short of intercourse. Your period and male pleasuring are not mutually exclusive.

Let's be clear about this. Men would prefer that in a sexual encounter, you and he are equally satisfied. But if biology or timing don't allow for your complete pleasure, no man is thinking, *Oh, if she can't have it, then I shouldn't have it, either.* Any man that tells you that is a complete and pathetic liar. Whether it's selfish or not, sensitive or insensitive, men still want to be taken care of even during your time of the month. They want you to know this, but they won't tell you, because they don't want to be branded as selfish and not caring. In the previous example, Lisa won the day in the second scenario, because her actions let Michael know that she knows what he wants and she's still willing to contribute, even though the physical pleasure might not be equally shared. What's even more compelling is that your man might not say this, but rest assured he will gratefully remember that you were willing to take care of him although you couldn't be taken care of yourself. These are valuable points that you can redeem later and he'll be happy to oblige.

THE SITUATION

The night is going great. The guy you've been dating has once again taken you to a wonderful dinner and filled you up not just with delicious cuisine but stimulating conversation. Things have been progressing rather smoothly in your relationship, and you've been most appreciative of his patience. This has been so different from most of the guys you've dated who were trying to rip your clothes off after the second date.

One night you go out for a drink after dinner and before you know it, you're hugging and kissing and feeling really good. You suggest that it's time go home before you get arrested for indecent exposure. All the way home in the back of the taxi you can't keep your hands off each other. You barely make it inside of your apartment before the clothes start coming off. He is a tremendous kisser, and tonight he's the best he's ever been.

You're in the bed, clothes off, hotter than a Brazilian sun, and you just want it to happen. Tonight *is* the night. You bring him on top of you, because it's time. You want him now! You can feel on your thigh that he's definitely ready. Then it happens. You realize that he hasn't taken out a condom, and things are getting really close—too close actually. Not wanting to ruin the moment, you whisper to him, "Do you have something?" He tells you he doesn't, but it just so happens that you have several condoms in the top drawer of your night stand and they're within arm's reach. You want to get one right away and not kill the mood. But then you have second thoughts. What will he think of you when he finds out you have your own supply of condoms lying around? *So now what do you do?*

(See The Handle #2)

Being Adventurous Is Advantageous

Here's an unspoken rule when it comes to men and sex. We want you to be somewhat freaky in the privacy of the bedroom or wherever we decide to do the deed. Freaky is not a negative term by any stretch of the imagination. If it still doesn't feel right, you can say kinky, adventurous, or open-minded. All of these convey the message that men want more than just the missionary position when the lights are turned off. We want creativity, a little daring, some verbal banter, and willingness to find new ways to bring us to arousal and ultimate satisfaction. Does this mean you have to venture into S & M or swing with other couples? Absolutely not. What it means is that repeatedly doing it the same way with the same level of intensity is flat-out boring and an excuse for us to seek others to fulfill some of our fantasies.

My women friends have confided in me that they are unwilling to experiment with their man because they feel like participating in novelty makes them sexually abnormal or, even worse, a whore. Rest easy, you reluctant ones: nothing could be further from the truth. First of all, while your girlfriends might not admit to it, more of them than you think are trying new things with their men in private. Also, you are an adult. It is completely fine for two adults to engage in adventurous physical intimacy as long as both parties consent, and it doesn't veer off into the extreme with one of the parties feeling uncomfortable or regretting the decision. Men want this variety in their relationships. Men have fantasies—not all of them should be fulfilled—but they want you to know that they would like to try something different and they don't always want to be the one to introduce it into the relationship. They want *you* to be the initiator at least some of the time. Always having to be the one to make a suggestion or get something started, even though you might go along with it, becomes tiresome and eventually disappointing.

Which brings us to one of the biggest ways that lead to a mutually satisfying sex life—spontaneity. **What your man wants you to know but won't tell you is that it's not always the physical act of sex that he finds gratifying; your willingness to do it impulsively at unexpected times or in unexpected places can be a thrill in itself.** I was having dinner recently with several men and the conversation got around to sex—surprise, surprise. After covering a lot of ground, one of my friends spoke about how satisfied he was in his current relationship, because the woman he was dating was willing to do it outside of the bedroom. They did it in the backseat of a car after pulling over on a weekend drive to the country. They did it in a secluded bathroom in a club he belonged to where they were having dinner. They did it against a rock on one of their hiking trips. The rest of us listened to every detail, and what most captured our attention and imaginations was the description of where they chose to do the deed and how impulsivity had been the driving force simply because one or both of them got the urge.

Men are more than happy to do it in traditional places like the bedroom and shower, but being impulsive in timing and location can add sizzle to what might be an otherwise bland sexual relationship. Your man is even willing to carry the brunt of decision-making when it comes to choosing these alternative places, but be ready to accommodate and sometimes take ownership of coming up with new places. I'm not saying you need to do wacky things like having sex in the back of a church, but there is something to be said about the element of danger when it comes to sex. Some men might be turned on by a woman with 36 double-Ds and a tiny waist, while for others it might be having sex in a place where you might get caught. If you don't have stunning physical attributes (and not many women do—at least not naturally!), you can be equally successful at turning on your man by mixing up the environment and timing of your sexual encounters.

> **In an international survey, 41% of men said that their partners don't know about their sexual fantasies.**
>
> Source: The Great Male Survey, 2010, Askmen.com

Keep Some of Your Clothes On

One mistake most couples make is thinking that having sex means having to strip off all of their clothes and jump in the sack. This is definitely appropriate if you plan on having an all-out romp with a lot of position changes and explorations, but it doesn't always have to be this way. **What your man wants you to know but won't tell you is that keeping some of your clothes on can be even more of a turn-on than full nudity.** Once again, occasionally dispensing with the traditional can be a welcome and exciting change. What's even better is that it can be so simple to execute. When some women hear, "Let's try something different" or "Let's change up the routine," they get nervous, thinking our next request will involve devices and paraphernalia. Not so.

If you took a poll of male sexual fantasies, one of the most common is taking a woman in a tight dress or skirt, turning her around against the wall or over a piece of furniture, and taking off her blouse and bra but leaving her in the dress and

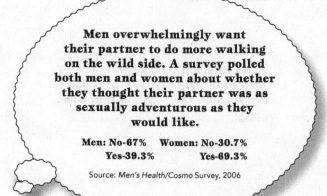

Men overwhelmingly want their partner to do more walking on the wild side. A survey polled both men and women about whether they thought their partner was as sexually adventurous as they would like.

Men: No-67%   Women: No-30.7%
Yes-39.3%   Yes-69.3%

Source: *Men's Health/Cosmo* Survey, 2006

heels. There is something extremely sexy and naughty about doing it partially clothed. Even something as simple as taking off all of your clothes, but leaving on an unbuttoned shirt so that it falls partially open can drive men completely crazy.

We are well aware that your clothes can be quite expensive and that certain fabrics are difficult to clean, so you might find yourself in a bit of a pickle between letting us live out our fantasy at that moment and trying to save yourself a ruined garment or heavy dry-cleaning bill. If it really matters that much to you, then by all means take off whatever it is that's worrying you, but do it before things go too far. The worst thing for men is to get in a groove only to find you're distracted by what is happening or might happen to your blouse or skirt. If garment preservation is a priority, participate in some "pre-action." Then, when the intensity turns up a notch, quickly shed without ruining the mood or flow.

Too Much Is Really Too Much

I titled this chapter Be a Freak but Not a Freak of the Week because there is a *huge* difference. A "freak" is willing to walk a little on the wild side, but within bounds. A "freak of the week" either walks too far on the wild side or goes there too often. Let me give you an example: A freak might occasionally entertain a ménage à trois, but a freak of the week will entertain a ménage à trois with her best friend in the threesome. **What your man wants you to know but won't tell you is that he wants you to be a little naughty and edgy, but going too far can be a real turn-off.**

Men might talk a big game about wanting a woman who will do anything, anywhere, but the truth is if they get this type of partner, they are not likely to remain in an exclusive, long-term relationship. Men simply think that if you're willing to do ridiculously wild things, such as having sex in a public place or swinging with another couple, you've done it before and had too many partners. It's not that your man expects you to be a virgin. In fact, most men want a woman with some experience because they can avoid all of the teaching and patience that's required to bring a neophyte up to speed. But if you're someone who's regularly swinging from a steel bar hanging from the ceiling of your bedroom wearing studded leather, your man might enjoy the role-playing, but he's also wondering whether your proclivity toward the risqué means you'll be stepping out of the relationship if he doesn't consistently share your appetite for the kinky stuff.

Tens of thousands of men were given choices of which sexual act they most fantasize about engaging in with their partner. The results:

A threesome: 34%
Anal sex: 19%
Sex in public: 15%

Source: The Great Male Survey, 2010, Askmen.com

You're making a big mistake if you think going to extremes is going to keep your man from looking at other women. Men are *always* going to look at other women. Once again, it's a DNA thing. What you need to worry about, however, is whether your man goes beyond just looking and finds it necessary to engage. It's the engagement part, not the looking, that becomes disrespectful and unacceptable. Being a freak of the week will eventually push your man away to the point where he looks for someone who's willing to try different things—but *only* with him. He wants to be assured that what you're doing is special for him and not something that you are willing to do with anyone who springs for a movie and nice dinner. Just like women, men like to feel special and unique. Your man wants you to know this, but he won't tell you for fear of appearing weak or too emotional.

Physical intimacy is one of the most alluring aspects of a relationship. It's not the *only* thing that must be in alignment for success, but rarely is it possible to land and keep your man if you can't satisfy him sexually. Yes, there are men who have outrageous libidos. Plenty of men are also habitual womanizers even while they're in committed relationships. That's the 5 percent of the male population you wouldn't want anyway. The average, decent guy, however, is quite willing to enter a monogamous relationship, but he's almost certainly unwilling to do so if his sexual needs are not met. I don't care what expert advice the magazine columnists preach, a man will leave you or be unfaithful the quickest when he finds himself stuck in an unhealthy sexual relationship that shows no signs of improving. Men want you to want sex and they also want you to enjoy it. While it might sometimes seem like your man is content with you doing all the giving and him the receiving, that is far from the truth. Men are a lot more sexually egalitarian than we're given credit. We want you to feel fulfilled so that the pleasure is mutual. The problem is that most men won't tell you this, and they typically won't take the next step of asking you what makes you feel good. Everyone is different. What excites one person doesn't necessarily excite another. One of the biggest gratifications of our sexual ego is to be successful in turning you on and making you want more. We want and often need you to tell us what it will take to give you ultimate satisfaction.

Top Five Mood Killers

1. **Stinky Breath.** There's absolutely no need to have bad breath. There are endless types of breath fresheners

in your local deli, gas station, or grocery store. At any hour of the night you can find a product to keep you fresh. If you have to choose something to "not leave home without," ditch the American Express card but don't forget the mints.

2. **Pesky Pets.** Animals are awesome. You won't get any argument from us about that. But animals are *not* awesome when they are staring at us like they're going to attack if we don't take our hands off of your asset. Even worse is when they want to sit on the couch or in bed with us. Either put little Cocoa in the bathroom or take us into another room where we can close the door and not be interrupted.

3. **Granny Panties.** These are unacceptable, especially given today's expansive variety of lingerie. With so many undergarment options around, you don't need to wear what looks like something you borrowed from Grandma's drawer. Seriously. I'm not saying you have to go to Victoria's Secret and spend a small fortune, but please wear something that looks like it comes from the last decade. Big, wide cotton panties with floral prints just aren't gonna work. Your undies are just as important as your clothes, and sometimes even more so. There's nothing worse than a great ass in tight jeans being ruined by the wrong panty lines.

4. **"I don't have any condoms, and I'm not on the pill."** Really? Does this have to be said when we're lying butt naked in bed and almost in? You've been going

at it for at least half an hour, starting back on your couch, and you've made it to the bed and "the moment" is upon us. And now you want to reveal that you don't have any condoms *and* you're not on the pill? Talk about instant *de*-rection. Bingo. I admit that it's completely my fault for not being prepared with a condom, but I didn't think things would get this far. It's not that what you just said isn't important for us to know, but please choose a better time to discuss it so that we can plan accordingly.

5. **Ringing Cell Phones.** All of us are digitally connected these days—that's just part of modern life. In fact, it's mind-boggling to imagine how our parents even lived without cell phones, PDAs, and instant-messaging software. But there comes a time to disconnect. Talk about breaking the rhythm. There's nothing worse than a shocking ring that screams out in the dark. Turning the cell phone to vibrate isn't much better as it dances across the nightstand like someone on crutches trying to do the tango. Turn the damn thing off so we can focus on the matter at hand.

THE HANDLE #2

Don't reach for your condoms! This move could prove to be a big mistake, regardless of how much either of you wants to go further. This situation requires some quick thinking. If you have told him in the past that you always have condoms lying around, or that you were going out to buy some for the both of you, it's completely fine to reach for them. If not, then the safe play is to calmly and politely refuse to go any further until he brings condoms.

Reaching into your own supply of condoms can send the wrong signal. If he doesn't know you have them, he might wonder why you have an inventory of condoms just lying around. Are they from a previous relationship? If so, that's kind of icky. Having condoms at the ready makes him wonder how often a similar situation arises when you need protection because he's forgotten his.

Having emergency condoms is a completely good idea. In the heat of the moment, anything can happen, and you don't want to be in a situation where you go further without protection. Make it clear to your partner long before you get into this situation that it is your policy to keep condoms just in case the need arises. Once he knows that you have them, his mind won't start wandering in the wrong direction when he's in need and you suddenly produce one. It's all about the 5 Ps: Proper preparation prevents poor performance.

CHEAT SHEET

WHAT YOU KNOW *NOW*

Men don't always need to hit a home run to relieve their sexual tension or have a good time. Sometimes just a base hit will do.

Even though it's that time of the month, men still have certain needs and would appreciate it if you could satisfy them.

It's not always the physical act of sex that men find gratifying, but your willingness to do it impulsively, at the least expected times or in the least expected places.

Keeping some of your clothes on can be even more of a turn-on.

Men want you to be a little naughty and edgy, but going too far can be a real turn-off.

NEVER go all the way on the first few dates, even if your man says he wants it and is trying his best to get there. Give him something to savor and a reason to want more later.

Be willing to try different sexual experiences, but up to a point. It's okay to say no to your man's suggestions some of the time, but not all of the time.

Tell your man what makes you feel most sexually fulfilled. Use clear, detailed language, and even demonstrate if necessary.

Stinky breath, meddlesome pets, granny panties, last-second birth control conversations, and singing phones are complete mood-killers.

THE
THIRD

MEAN WHAT YOU SAY OR DON'T SAY IT

*Relationships shouldn't be like spy games with all kinds of
misdirection and subterfuge. It's a dangerous gamble to assume
that your partner is going to read between the lines and walk
away with the intended message rather than the one you've
actually given. If you want us to know something, sometimes it's
better just to go ahead and say it.*

QUITE OFTEN THE success of a relationship—the ones that are
just starting as well as the ones that have been going on
for a while—rises and falls with the quality of communication
between partners. Men for the most part are very concrete individuals, who often see things in black and white. This makes
our world simple, and we also like simplicity in our relationships. Whether this is good or bad, right or wrong, doesn't really
matter. It is what it is and it's unlikely you're going to "teach"
your man how to see that there's a color called gray. So don't
waste your time waiting for your man to develop a skill you

possess in abundance—reading between the lines. Say what you mean or don't say it at all.

Mind Reading Is an Overrated Art

One of the biggest mistakes a woman makes when trying to get her man to do something she wants is to expect him to read her mind. Forget it. If what you want is important to you, taking the direct path is a lot more effective than making us guess. **What your man wants you to know but won't tell you is to stop all the reverse psychology and say what it is you really want**. Here's an example of how things go wrong:

VALERIE: What color should I get? *(Valerie holds up two shirts, one blue and one white.)*

MARK: Hmmm. I like the blue one.

VALERIE: But white goes with everything and I can wear it more often.

MARK: But you already have a lot of white shirts.

VALERIE: Yeah, but none like this. They're all different.

MARK: *(Sighs).* A lot of them seem the same to me. I like the blue shirt.

VALERIE: I have this great skirt that will go with the white one. The blue won't work.

MARK: Okay, get the white one.

VALERIE: Maaaaaaark, you're just saying that because you don't want to help me.

MARK: No, I'm saying that because you asked me my opinion and I gave it to you, and then you argued me down about it, so I'll just give you the answer you want to hear.

VALERIE: Forget it, Mark. I can tell it really doesn't matter to you. Why do you have to make everything so difficult?

This conversation and variations of it are played out millions of times a day as we are asked our opinion under the guise that what we think might actually matter. The truth, however, is that you've already made up your mind, and you want us to read your mind so that we can second your unrevealed decision. **What your man wants you to know but won't tell you is that he is a horrible mind reader, and he doesn't want to deal with the complications of reading your mind anyway.** We have absolutely no shame in admitting that we are extremely nearsighted in many respects, and if you consider that a weakness, then that's all right, too. But you're making a huge mistake when you expect us to be able to see things out of our field of vision.

When our opinion doesn't match your opinion or a decision you've already made, the result is all kinds of problems. The solution is simple: If you are making a decision and truly leaning in one direction, go ahead and ask us our opinion, but make sure you tell us which way you're already leaning. This will avoid a lot of unnecessary drama and make us feel like our input really matters. Maybe we can add some new information or a different perspective that can help you make the decision. We want to feel like what we're saying has some impact and real value to your process. Be honest up-front about where you stand, and the next time you ask for our opinion we'll be happy to give it in an honest way. If you're looking for a rubber stamp, we can do that, too, but much prefer you seek it from your girlfriends instead! They read between the lines much better than we do, and they are much better at figuring out what you really want to hear.

Don't Call Me, but I Want You to Call Me

I was sitting at Starbucks one day waiting for a friend to arrive when two women sat down next to me. They looked to be in their upper twenties, were well dressed, rather attractive, and completely hip in the way city girls tend to be. I wasn't trying to eavesdrop on their conversation, but their table was close to mine and there wasn't much noise in the store at the time, so I couldn't help but hear what they were saying. It went something like this.

WOMAN 1: I am so pissed at Luke.

WOMAN 2: What happened?

WOMAN 1: We got into a huge fight a few days ago and I haven't heard from him since.

WOMAN 2: What were you fighting about?

WOMAN 1: He wanted to go to the movies and I wanted to go shopping first. He didn't want to go shopping with me, but wanted me to meet him at the movies. And I was like, no, I want to spend the day together. Going shopping with me for an hour isn't gonna kill you.

WOMAN 2: It's always about what they want to do. No compromise.

WOMAN 1: That's what I told him. Relationships are about compromise and sometimes doing stuff you may not want to do.

WOMAN 2: What did he say to that?

WOMAN 1: That he does compromise, but going shopping
is something he hates, and why would I want to drag
him into stores when I know he hates it. Then we
got into a big argument. I got so upset that I told him
not to call me until he grew up.

WOMAN 2: Has he called you?

WOMAN 1: Not for three days. Can you believe it? Every
time the phone rings I hope it's him. I want to talk to
him. Even though he was completely a jerk about
going shopping, I miss him. Should I call him?

WOMAN 2: Never! That means he won and you gave in.
You have to stand up to him.

WOMAN 1: But I can't stop thinking about him. I can't
stop wondering who he's talking to and what he's
doing. It's driving me crazy.

This is a classic relationship hot spot and it doesn't need to
be. Granted, everyone says things sometimes in the heat of the
moment that they don't mean. But while you might not mean
what you say, you ultimately have to take responsibility for it.
Even though your man has made you really angry about a particular issue and you need some space to cool down and gather
yourself, the worst thing you can do is tell him not to call you.
**What your man wants you to know but won't tell you is
that if you're having an argument and you tell him not to
call you, then depending on how upset he is, that's exactly what he's going to do, because he knows it's going
to piss you off even more.** In the continued spirit of transparency, let me tell you that sometimes we know damn well that
you really don't mean what you've just said, and we'll give you

some cooling-off time before we go ahead and call you anyway. But other times we get upset ourselves and have finally had enough, so we just say, "Okay, she doesn't want me to call her, so I won't." Now it's a pissing contest, and the truth is that our arc can go a lot farther than yours. Biological fact. You're now in a game you're unlikely to win, and the consequences will not be what you want.

Why even introduce this kind of trouble into the relationship? If you really want to talk to your man but you're upset with him and just need a cooling-off period, then tell him so. Better yet, tell him how you feel and that you'll call him when you've gotten over whatever it is that is causing the dissention. This way you still get the break that you need, but you are now in control of when the contact resumes, and it's no longer a pissing contest. Telling your man not to call you is really playing dating roulette. He might disregard what you say and call you out of guilt or a willingness to smooth things over, but there's going to come a time when he really takes what you say to heart and doesn't call you. That's when you've reached an impasse that can have detrimental and long-term consequences.

You Don't Have to Come Over

My roommate had a girlfriend once who came down with a cold maybe once a month. In the middle of summer with the temperature threatening triple digits, she still found a way to catch a cold. And her colds weren't just her sneezing now and again. They were full-blown, puffy-eyed, red-nosed, my-head-feels-like-it's-going-to-explode colds. When she got them she was understandably miserable, but she had her own way of dealing with them, which involved drinking some concoction her grandmother had taught her how to make and popping a bunch of supplements that she said boosted her immune system.

Several months into the relationship my roommate began to understand that when she said, "Don't come over," she really was saying, "I really want you to come over, but I don't want you to come if you don't want to." The first few times she had one of her cold spells and told him not to come over, he simply didn't. He thought she was being considerate and didn't want him to catch a nasty cold. What sense did it make to have both of them battling that stubborn little rhinovirus? Then one time she had a cold and he offered to bring her some soup and freshly squeezed orange juice. Out of nowhere she snapped at him, "Why are you offering that now? You didn't offer to come be with me the last time I felt like this."

Whoa! Where did that come from? The last couple of times she insisted that he not come over, so he thought he was respecting her wishes. When people are sick, sometimes they like to be left alone. Now all of a sudden he's being brought up on charges for something that happened a couple of months ago for viola-

5 THINGS YOUR MAN WANTS TO HEAR

"What can I do to make you feel good?"
"I love your [mention body part]."
"You look so good in that!"
"Okay, I'll give it a try."
"I really need your advice on this."

tions he didn't even know existed. This led to a long and contentious conversation. She told him that if he knew she was sick (which he did), he should've come over regardless of what she said—without even asking her if she wanted him to be with her. He should've just showed up on his own to offer her comfort. That is probably true. Sometimes it makes a person feel a lot better when you take the initiative. No argument there. But when you tell someone that they don't have to come over, you've muddied the waters. We are taking you at your word when in reality we shouldn't, and now we've landed in hot water we didn't even know was there in the first place.

Make it easy on both of us. **What your man wants you to know but won't tell you is that he actually enjoys coming to your rescue, even if his reasons are somewhat selfish**. If you want us to come over, whether it's because you're sick or had a bad day at work and need someone to lean on, that's not a problem. Believe me, if you give us any indication that you want us there, we'll be there in a flash with flowers in hand and all kinds of other goodies. Yes, we want you to feel better, but also know that we like to swoop in and save the day. It's our superhero complex, something that we develop as little boys playing with our action figures and watching caped crusaders rescue the damsel in distress.

Don't Get Me Anything Big (Yeah, Right)

These are the famous last words of complicated gift-giving in a relationship. Think about how many times you may have said to someone you're dating, "Oh, don't go to too much trouble. Just get me something simple, nothing big." Now think about how many times you've been disappointed at the gift you did or didn't receive after making that statement. *Well, I really didn't think that he was going to actually take me seriously.* Gift-giving can be one of the most complicated and angst-provoking aspects of any relationship, especially one in its infancy when you're just getting to know each other. The good news is that it really doesn't have to be so stressful, especially if you follow some basic rules. The bad news is that most people don't know or choose to ignore the basic rules.

What your man wants you to know but won't tell you is that he's willing to give you the gift you want (within limits), but be honest about what you really want. Don't make the guy you're dating think that a really nice dinner is enough for a special occasion when really you want the nice dinner *and* a Louis Vuitton handbag with all of those shiny gold buckles. You are often very good at hiding your disappointment if the gift doesn't meet your expectations, but the disappointment is there nonetheless. Then you tend to hold on to it and express it at another time when we can't make the connection that your outburst or foul mood has nothing to do with what's happening now but rather the gift we gave you some time ago that you didn't like.

What you need to understand is that we really are suckers when it comes to wanting to make you happy with gifts. Our experience has selfishly taught us that a nice gift can lead to a lot of things that we will enjoy tremendously. Men may not always get it, but we are quick to learn when something we do or say brings the results we're seeking. The right gift—and that doesn't necessarily mean the most expensive—makes you feel special, and when you feel special we can earn some redeemable points. It's not lost on us that women like to show off to one another what their man has given them. There are many reasons why we are willing to go the distance in the gifting department, but don't lead us down a false path by telling us it's no big deal when really it is.

There is definitely an art to gifting, especially early in a relationship. What you have to understand is that in our minds gifting should more or less follow an exponential curve—slow to start but fast to finish. Don't expect or ask your man to start off by purchasing elaborate, expensive gifts right from the beginning. I remember a young basketball player who had gone to Yale and came from a wealthy family. It had been widely rumored around camp that he had received a Mercedes-Benz on his sixteenth birthday when he got his driver's license. While some of the other counselors were understandably envious, I remember an older counselor's words: *The worst thing about getting that car at sixteen is, where do you go from there?* The same question applies to early gifting in relationships. If we buy you that knock-you-outta-your-socks gift right away, then where do we go from there? Let your expectations and requests build throughout the relationship so both of us will avoid the classic awkward gift moment and resulting disappointment. Men are hugely appreciative of women who don't place a priority on the expense of a gift. In fact, what you probably don't know is that the less you expect the more we want to give you.

THE SITUATION

You've been dating a great guy for six months. He is the best boyfriend that you've ever had, especially after a string of real losers. He has everything you want in a man and then some. He has an exceptional moral compass and was raised in a solid middle-class family with strong values and a deep sense of social responsibility. You have even talked to your girlfriends about how you could one day see yourself standing next to him at the altar. This is just the kind of guy he is—a real keeper.

He has also let you in on his thoughts and fears like no other man ever has. He's emotionally honest, and his vulnerabilities, while there are only a few, make you even more attracted to him. He has told you about the failures of past relationships and was forthright about his contributions. He had caught his last girlfriend cheating on him and it destroyed him for over a year, and even now as he recounts what happens, you can tell the scab has fallen off, but the wound is still pink.

He invites you out to dinner at one of your favorite restaurants. You have a good time laughing at family stories and planning a vacation together—your first big one. He has gone to great lengths to ensure that everything is just so, even consulting his female friends to make sure he hasn't forgotten anything. His sensitivity is one of his most endearing qualities.

That night he walks you to your door, and normally he would come in for a little nightcap, but the next morning he has to catch an early train for an out-of-town meeting. He kisses you long and hard, and you feel yourself getting all warm in those special places. After what you both agree will be the last kiss, he stares deep into your eyes, almost like he's looking into your soul, and says, "I love you." You like him a lot. A whole lot. In fact, you might even love him, but you're not sure yet. Everything is so right where you want it to be. He has all you want in a man, but you're not sure about the love thing just yet. It feels like a thousand thoughts and scenarios have flown through your mind in that two-second pause before you suddenly realize he's waiting for your response. *So now what do you do?*

(See The Handle #3)

Sex Lies Always Backfire

Men have earned quite a bawdy reputation when it comes to sex and, to be honest, we completely deserve it. We *love* sex. We *love* physical pleasure. We *love* being able to demonstrate our sexual prowess. We *love* to be told that we are spectacular in the sack. **But what your man wants you to know but won't tell you is that he *doesn't love* sex lies**.

Men have rather large sex egos. (Surprise, surprise.) We want to prove more to ourselves than to you that we can make magic with our equipment. Even those of us who are genetically disadvantaged still believe we can make fireworks if we work it right. Unfortunately, much of our male identity is centered around what's behind the zipper and the degree to which we can prove that we are worthy of our XY designation. I'm not looking for any sympathy here, but the truth is that the pressure on us is at times overwhelming, so much so that we do really stupid things and think really stupid thoughts and make really stupid decisions. I don't care how small or big or cool or hyper or whatever your man is, he wants to sexually satisfy you. This is the part that most women completely get, but what you don't get is that we don't want false verification. Sooner or later the truth will come out, whether you tell us, or we hear it from someone you've "confided in," or we figure it out by ourselves. The pain we feel from learning the truth behind your sex lies is greater than the pleasure we get from your confirmation of our skill.

If your man isn't exactly doing it for you in the sack, it can be an opportunity to make lemonade out of a lemon. You might think that he would be embarrassed by your bringing up some aspects of his technique that he could improve, but **what your man wants you to know but won't tell you is that he wants you to tell him what he can do better or differently to sexually satisfy you**. Yes, we would be extremely gratified if right from the beginning we could figure out on our own what turns you on and makes you get the most out of an intimate encounter. But sometimes we just aren't making the right connection and what we think is working for you really isn't. It does neither of us any good for you to pretend like everything is fine and no adjustments need to be made. Eventually pretense will blow up in our faces. Meanwhile, you'll continue to suffer needlessly to the point that you'll begin to resent the sexual aspect of the relationship and either start losing interest or seek satisfaction elsewhere. When this happens we both lose and the relationship, which could've been rewarding and lasting with a little open communication and tweaking, is not likely to survive.

What ticks us off most is the misperception many women have about our desperate need to bring them to climax, even if it means faking it. While your intentions are thoughtful and caring, **what your man wants you to know but won't tell you is that when it comes to faking orgasms, thank you, but no thank you**. Yes, our ego is all wrapped up in our sexual performance, and we know you're trying not to hurt our feelings, but sex is an area where we want the straight truth. We're not so "sexocentric" that you need to lie to us. It's like a guy who goes out and plays golf by himself—and cheats! He can report a false score to his friends, but he knows the real truth and can't escape it regardless of how creative his imagination. The same thing applies to knowing the truth about sex. Yes, we want to sit at the bar with our guy friends and brag about bringing you to orgasm three times in one session, but most of

> **According to a recent survey, 85% of men reported their partner had an orgasm at the most recent event; however, only 64% of women said that they actually had one.**
>
> Source: National Survey of Sexual Health and Behavior, Indiana University, 2010

the time we know when the orgasms are fake and we can't elude that simple truth, regardless of how much our creative imaginations embellish the experience to our male compadres. The indignity deep inside can't be overcome by the impression we think we're making on our friends.

The Right Talk Makes a Difference

Good communication is the foundation of any solid relationship, and the first layer of that foundation is honesty. Sometimes the truth hurts, but at the end of the day it typically works out much better than telling us what you might consider a little white lie. It's not that we men always want to hear bad news or that our feelings can't be hurt, but we will suck up our medicine regardless of how awful it might taste. Telling us what you think we want to hear might work for the moment, but if what you say is at odds with the truth eventually you'll either have to continue to lie or come clean. It's the coming clean that is often more difficult than just being honest up front. **What your man wants you to know but won't tell you is that he appreciates your concern for his feelings, but if you have something to say that you're keeping quiet because you're afraid of hurting or angering him, go ahead and open up with the truth. Do it in a way that gets your point across but doesn't eviscerate him or make him feel like a complete loser.**

We are very realistic when it comes to the ups and downs of life. In fact, we learn at an early age—whether from sports, first crushes, or relationships with our fathers—that nothing in life is perfect. We may *want* things to be perfect, but we know that perfection is impossible to achieve. Relationships are much stronger when we are comfortable enough to share the bad times as well as the good times. Don't shield your man from something that you might think will reflect poorly on you. I'm not saying that he needs to know every little detail of everything that has happened or is happening in your life. But keeping secret a major issue could make him think when you finally reveal it that you didn't trust him or your relationship enough to share it.

One of the biggest communication mistakes that people make in relationships is thinking that everything should be stored away in silos, with access based on the importance of the contents the silos contain. A successful relationship is not built by sharing only the aspects you consider important or noteworthy. Talking about even the most trivial of things—the funny hat you saw a man wear while pumping his gas—can add texture to a relationship. It's shortsighted to think that we only want to hear about the forecasted drop in the stock market or the promotion you might be close to earning at work. The fullness of life and relationships means sharing things that are funny or sad as well as boring or wildly exciting. Relationships are much more enjoyable when they have multiple gears, when you can talk openly and honestly about all kinds of experiences that have impacted you in some way.

One communication skill can't be overrated—listening. While men are fine with your generating the bulk of the conversational flow, we are not fine when we feel as though your talking becomes an obstacle to your listening. The best communicators are the best listeners. Conversations are two-way streets. Unfortunately, when you are either extremely excited about something or red with rage, you can get so caught up in telling the story or expressing your emotions that you either don't give us room to contribute or don't listen to what we say when we do get a chance to squeeze in a comment. One of the biggest complaints that we have about our partners or potential partners is that we don't feel like you're really listening to what we're saying.

Sometimes you don't even realize you're being dismissive. Our beef is not that you disagree with what we have to say; we don't want or expect you to rubber-stamp everything. It's *how* you disagree that makes a big difference. For example, we present a plan of action for a certain problem and once we're done, the first thing you do is point out everything that is wrong with the plan. That drives us mad as hell. Here's a better way of getting your point across without alienating or infuriating us, a strategy that works unbelievably well: Start off with what you find agreeable in our analysis, i.e., the common ground. Once you've hit the positive notes, then slide into where your opinion differs. Responding with your disagreements first not only backs us up on our heels, it makes us feel like you weren't really listening to what we said, or that you heard only what you wanted to hear.

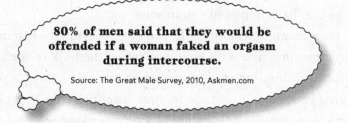

80% of men said that they would be offended if a woman faked an orgasm during intercourse.

Source: The Great Male Survey, 2010, Askmen.com

Men are looking for women who are honest, considerate, and great communicators. We also want to believe that when we expose our weaknesses you will not look down on us or throw them back in our face in the future. It might sound like a cliché, but there's truly nothing more reassuring in a relationship than when actions speak louder than your words. Giving us the full you, even if that sometimes is not a pleasant experience, is much better than giving us only selected parts you think we can handle.

THE HANDLE #3

If you don't love him, the last thing you want to say is, "I love you, too." This might help you slide out of the awkward situation you now find yourself in, but it is likely to give rise to myriad issues. When it comes to "I love you," honesty is definitely the best policy, even if you think not saying it might hurt his feelings a little.

Here are some suggestions for getting out of this situation without hurting his feelings or lying about your own. My favorite: "I'm falling in love with you, too." This is an excellent response as it is not an outright "I don't love you." Instead, it is hopeful and shows that you are committed and in the process of reaching that emotional place where he already seems to be. Saying this with excitement and some kind of display of affection is a very acceptable response without causing hurt feelings.

Another response is to be in receptive awe of his statement. "Oh my God, that is so sweet. You are totally going to make me cry right now. I am so happy we are together and things are going well. This relationship is making me feel so good." You have not lied about whether you love him, but you have at least given him hope that his love is wanted and accepted and that the overall relationship is valuable. Focusing on how great you feel about the relationship is effective, because it prevents you from having to address the love part of it. He might want to hear you proclaim love and be disappointed that it's not in your response, but this disappointment can be lessened if you're effusive about how important he is to you.

Sometimes it's not easy to be honest and sensitive of someone's feelings at the same time, but the pain of not having someone return an admission of love is a lot less than the pain of discovering that the person lied and never loved you in the first place. Men would much rather endure the pain of unrequited love than the pain of deception.

THE CHEAT SHEET

WHAT YOU KNOW *NOW*

Stop all the reverse psychology and say what you really want.

Men are horrible mind readers and don't want to deal with the complications of reading your mind, anyway.

If you and your man are having an argument and you tell him not to call you, then, depending on how upset he is, that's exactly what he's going to do because he knows it's going to piss you off even more.

Men actually enjoy coming to your rescue, even if the reasons are somewhat selfish.

Men are willing to give you the gift you want (within limits), but be honest about what you *really* want.

Men don't love sex lies.

Men want you to tell them what they can do better or differently to sexually satisfy you.

When it comes to faking orgasms, thank you, but no thank you.

Men appreciate your concern for their feelings, but if you have something to say that you're withholding because you're afraid of hurting or angering them, go ahead and open up with the truth.

THE
FOURTH

SHELL OUT THE CASH, SOME OF THE TIME

*A man's attraction to a woman's independence is totally
underrated. Acting like a woman doesn't mean you can't stand
on your own two feet. In fact, the vast majority of guys will
appreciate it.*

INDEPENDENCE IS ONE of the trickiest aspects of a relationship.
Not enough of it can be troublesome, and too much can make
you lonesome. Striking that balance can prove challenging and
time-consuming, but it can be one of the most important exercises you go through while establishing and maintaining a relationship. One of the first and major hurdles you'll likely face is
trying to understand what independence means to your man.
Once you leap across this hurdle, you have very little rest before you need to leap again, this time in your quest to figure out
how much. **What your man wants you to know but won't
tell you is that he wants you to need him, but only up to**

a point. He wants you to be able to stand on your own and have a life outside of your relationship. When you demonstrate this independence you let him know that, in the spirit of Tom Cruise in the movie *Jerry Maguire,* "you complete *him.*" There's something extremely sexy about a woman who can pay her own way and make her own decisions without feeling like she needs to check in first.

Showing Your Independence Doesn't Mean Chivalry Is Dead

Women often talk about being "treated like a woman," by which they mean us opening your car door, walking on the outside along the sidewalk to put ourselves between you and the street, and when dropping you off at home making sure you get through the door before we drive away. These old-fashioned courtesies require little effort, but they can have a large impact on your perception of how well mannered we are. But the classic bone of contention is money. Deciding who picks up the check has been one of the most polarizing issues between a man and a woman, especially when it comes to nascent relationships. We think that we have to pick up the check because you are going to judge how much of a gentleman we are based on our willingness to shell out the cash after dinner or before going into the movie theater. But this is something you need to understand. We don't want to pay because you expect us to; we prefer to pay because it's something we *want* to do.

A friend of mine who had made a significant amount of money and achieved a respectable level of fame went through a string of relationships in which he was not just the primary provider but the *only* provider. First-class plane tickets, five-star hotel tabs, shopping sprees in luxury stores—he put down his black card for all of it. In the beginning of each of these relationships he was more than happy to demonstrate to the women that he was able and willing to provide a certain lifestyle. But without fail, four or five months into the relationship, he tired of always footing the bill. It wasn't that he *needed* them to pick up the check at dinner every once in a while, but he wanted them to at least make the effort to demonstrate some independence and carry some of the load.

Then the craziest thing happened. He met a woman at an event and asked her out on a date. He was not aware of her financial situation. (That didn't matter to him anyway.) She was attractive and funny and very available. They had a great dinner that lasted for a couple of hours, with none of those typical first-date snags. When they walked outside to valet parking to get into their cars, he was shell-shocked when she slid behind the wheel of a car that was a lot more expensive and sleeker than his. Her car screamed at him, "Fuck your money, I've got my own." Then she tipped the valet a ten-spot and roared out of the driveway. My friend already liked her because of her looks, conversation, and humor, but now he really liked her because she could handle her business on her own and didn't need a damn thing from him other than companionship.

Please don't be mistaken. This is not an issue about who has the most money. It drives me crazy when I read relationship articles that say that men are intimidated by a woman who has a bigger bank account. Absurd. I've never met a man who said, "I don't want to date her because she has too much money." Anyone who believes men think like this are completely clueless. It's not how much money that matters to a man, but rather how you use your money. Independence is definitely more than just being able to pay your own way, but sometimes picking up the check makes a very bold statement to your man that you can make it without him. And this is something most men find attractive.

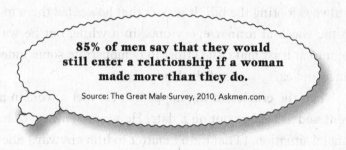

85% of men say that they would still enter a relationship if a woman made more than they do.

Source: The Great Male Survey, 2010, Askmen.com

Men Want You Shoulder-to-Shoulder, Not on Their Shoulders

Men want to be the center of your universe, but they don't want your universe to collapse if they don't talk to you for an entire day or see you for forty-eight hours. While hanging out with their friends, men don't want you waiting at home alone, anxiously watching the clock for their return. We want you to go out with your girlfriends and not worry about what we're doing— read: don't text us twenty times in the span of ten minutes, bombarding us with *So what are you up to?* We want you to miss us a little, but while we're away, push us to the back of your mind and focus on having fun with your friends. Later that night we can meet up, have a good romp, and go to bed peacefully.

What your man wants you to know but won't tell you is that proper spacing is not only fundamental to a good offense in basketball, it's also fundamental to successful relationships. What bothers the hell out of us is when we're made to feel almost guilty because we're doing something like going to a basketball game while you're home doing nothing, and you make a point of letting us know that you're doing nothing because we aren't home with you. When we tell you we're going to an after-work function, we want you to say, "No problem. I'm going to have drinks with the girls. Let's get together later, or maybe tomorrow." *That* is independence. *That* makes your man feel like he's not under pressure to be there all the time or that you are relying on him to prop up your social life. It's important to make it clear early in the relationship that you have your own set of friends and that although you think the world of him, there are times when you will do your own thing. Don't worry that he is going to interpret this as you don't want or enjoy his company. In fact, he is in complete agreement that there's nothing wrong with retreating to your own circle every once in a while and having a great time without him.

We completely get that a woman likes to be pampered and swept off her feet and all that jazz. But alarms start clanging in our heads when we begin to feel like we're becoming a babysitter. The constant need for attention or the need for us to "take care of things" can get tiresome very quickly and wear us down to the point that we start having serious second thoughts about the relationship. No man wants to feel like he's stuck at home looking after his kid sister because his parents had to go out to a party. It's important to be mindful that there are times when you might need to take out your own garbage or brush the snow off of your windshield. While the vast majority of the time these tasks should definitely be the responsibility of your man, occasionally doing for yourself will prevent him from feeling like you're a burden and, instead, make him want to do these things for you even more.

Be mindful of warning signs. If your man is consistently not wanting to help or tells you to do things without him, this could be a signal that things are not where they should be. Sticking with a lazy, selfish man is something you will regret. Be honest with yourself when making an assessment. If a gentle reminder or two doesn't lead to a reasonable change in his attitude or behavior, then cut the cord. He doesn't deserve you. There are plenty of single men out there who do.

THE SITUATION

You're on your first date with a guy you met while waiting for a girlfriend at Starbucks. You had struck up a conversation with him and found out that you had gone to the same college but had never met each other. He was a couple of years older and your college had more than twenty thousand undergraduates, so it's no surprise that you hadn't met before. You spent thirty minutes talking to him, and before he left he asked for your number, which you were happy to share.

That night you went on Facebook, found his page, and read up on him. He was the captain of the track team, vice president of his class, and had three sisters that look exactly like him. He had more than a thousand Facebook friends, and you even recognized a couple of them from some of your classes. He calls you the next day and you're really excited that he did. You haven't stopped thinking about him since he left Starbucks. You agree to have dinner Saturday night at a tapas restaurant—your choice.

The rest of the week you drive yourself crazy finding the right thing to wear and figuring out which way to style your hair. On the clothes front, you decide to go sexy but not trampy, and for your hair you decide to let it down with a lot of body. It's been several months since you've been on a date, so you have that nervous first-date energy going, especially since this guy seems like the real deal and you are totally attracted to him.

Dinner couldn't have gone any better. The conversation was natural and not forced. You have a lot in common and you make each other laugh. Before the entrée is served you are already relaxed and flirting. You really don't want the night to end. The waiter drops by and is about to place the check on the table when your date, currently in the middle of telling you about the best race he's ever run, stops in mid-sentence and says, "Two checks. Thanks." Then he goes back to the story without missing a beat. You're really not sure what just happened, but a couple of minutes later the waiter returns and places a check in front of him and one in front of you. Your date pulls out enough money to cover his check. He doesn't even look at yours or make any pretense of reaching across the table to pick it up. *So now what do you do?*

(See The Handle #4)

Ease the Holiday Burden

Surprisingly, a significant number of relationships are ruined during or right after the holidays. It's ironic that a time of celebration, when romance has a great opportunity to be enhanced, actually can become a time when relationships are severely damaged. One of the top causes? Expectations are too high. Men are notoriously lazy when it comes to planning gifts and romantic touches, such as weekend getaways. It doesn't mean we don't want to give you nice things and make you feel special, but the simple truth is that generally we're miserable at it, especially compared to you. I'm not saying we shouldn't try to do better and that you still shouldn't expect some level of effort, but don't put too much stock into where we took you for Valentine's Day or what we bought you for your birthday. I'm not saying that we should be let off the hook completely, but this is an area where being reasonable really counts.

Holidays can be a time of great pressure for men. We already know that you're going to do everything right. You'll find the right card with the right words. You'll find the perfect restaurant with the perfect ambience. You'll find just the right gift for us, because you've spent hours thinking about what we have and don't have and what we'd really like. **What your man wants you to know but won't tell you is that he would be extremely appreciative if you helped him by reducing some of the holiday pressure.** If you bring up the issue of gift-giving and holiday activities and tell him that it's all right to keep things simple right from the outset, then he will take a deep sigh of relief and not experience the angst that can come during these festive times.

Going too far the other way, however, can also be ineffective. He's not looking for you to have *no* expectations. Let him know

5   GIFTS YOU SHOULD AVOID GIVING

Clothes. (Unless your man has shown you exactly what he wants.)
Framed photographs. (Nice sentiment, but not in place of a gift. He's typically looking for something more substantial.)
Housewares. (Never. Ever.)
Food. (Home-cooked meals are great, but they should be part of the gift, not the entire gift.)
Books. (Only if it is autographed and personalized by someone he worships.)

that gifts don't have to be expensive, but they can be thoughtful. You can also let him know that the entire holiday doesn't have to be spent together, although you would like to spend at least some of it with him. Giving your man this kind of room will do wonders for your relationship and allow you to rack up some more redeemable points. I've had friends whose girlfriends have eased their holiday burden like this and, ironically, my friends ended up going all out, getting not just really thoughtful gifts but expensive ones. With the pressure gone, they were free to decide on their own how they wanted to celebrate the occasion.

Men completely understand the romance that surrounds certain holidays or special occasions, but reminding them of their obligations or criticizing what they've done or haven't done is a recipe for disaster. Your man will come to despise holidays and instead of participating with the intensity that you'd like him to have, he'll rebel or, even worse, drift away from you without telling you why. Of course there's a certain level of importance attached to certain holidays, but expecting too much can backfire. Try telling your man that since you both will be with your respective friends and families, you don't expect to talk as much over the holiday. Agree that checking in a couple of times—as long as those times are meaningful—will be enough until the holiday is over and you're back on track.

Two Places Are Much Better Than One

Unless we've fallen on prolonged financial hardship, most men don't want to live with their woman. **What your man wants you to know but won't tell you is that he wants you to have your spot and he wants to have his own.** Living together too early can be a big mistake. Sure, there can be some angst about what gets watched on the television—yet another episode of *Housewives* or *Sunday Night Football*—but the issue is much bigger than channel selection. Men need a cave they can crawl into and do what they want to do on their terms, even if that means just sitting on the couch for hours and playing the video games you find juvenile and unproductive.

There is absolutely nothing wrong with spending the night at his place or having him spend the night at yours. In a healthy relationship this will happen quite often, and your man is expecting and wanting that. **But what your man wants you to know but won't tell you is that he does not want you to have a key to his place.** Period. He might be willing to give you a key because you asked for one, but rest assured it's not because he had some deep desire to do so. (Of course, really long relationships and soon-to-be or engaged couples are an exception.) Think about the consequences he would face if he said no to your key request. He might be accused of wanting to have his apartment to himself so that he can usher in other women under the cover of darkness, or even worse, be charged with not loving you. Believe me, I've heard it all from my female friends. "If he loved me, then he'd give me a key to his apartment. What does it matter, I'm over to his place all the time anyway." It might be true that you spend a lot of time at his place, and he enjoys your being there, but we still have the feeling that as long as no one else has the key, our place is still our own and we control who enters and who doesn't. It's not about you.

Even if you live with a man, it's still important that you allow him his "man cave" if space permits. It's not that we don't enjoy spending time with you. It's not that we're not willing to watch HGTV and Food Network every once in a while with you. It's not that we don't want to cuddle on the sofa while you run your fingers through our hair. It's that some of the time we simply need to be alone in our space where we don't *want* to have a conversation about how our day went or what we plan on eating for dinner. Sometimes we come home from work or school and simply want to retreat into the quiet nothingness of our own four walls.

Where you live can also be an issue. Circumstances can force both men and women to live in arrangements that they otherwise would not choose, for example, living with parents or sharing a bedroom with a roommate. If you must live in a situation like this, there's not much you can do but work as hard as possible to improve your circumstances. Men are completely sympathetic to your position. **But what your man wants you to know but won't tell you is that it would make things a lot easier in your relationship if you had your own bedroom, one with a heavy door and a lock**.

Men can grow annoyed when we want to hook up for some private moments but hear, "We can't go to my place, because my roommate is home." Sure, we don't mind trekking back to our own spot, but after a while this imbalance in locations becomes tiresome. Sometimes we simply don't want to go back to our spot but prefer yours. One reason, which we won't tell you about because it's likely to cost us, is there are times when we just want to do our thing and afterward be free to get up and go. If we do it at your place, it's much easier to take leave on our own rather than doing it at our place, where it's impossible for us to tell *you* to go home. So you not having your own place backs us into a corner where we want to take care of business, but then we're faced with the obligatory post-coital interaction.

It is not the biggest crime in the world that we want to go

off and do our own thing. It's not that we're unemotional creatures, though I believe when it comes to sex, men are definitely less emotional about it than women—a DNA thing again. It's not that we think that you're a piece of meat and once we've had our fill we want to throw you away, or that we're only interested in the sex and not the "quality" time that couples spend together. It's just a basic part of our fabric, and trying to overanalyze it or draw conclusions from it will only lead you down a false path of misplaced assumptions. But when you don't have your own place to retreat to or where we can get intimate, you should be aware that the logistics of the physical relationship become more difficult and can make us feel like we're suffocating—something you never want us to feel.

Two Wheels Are Better Than Three in a Relationship

If you polled a thousand men about their biggest pet peeves in an evolving relationship I would bet half of what I own that one of the top three is the business of "third-wheeling." This drives us *absolutely* crazy, especially in the beginning when we're trying to establish a relationship. Think back to when kids learn how to ride a bicycle. Once the bike hierarchy is understood, every boy in the world wants to progress from a tricycle to a bicycle as fast as possible. There is a truly instructive lesson to be learned from this progression when it comes to understanding men.

What your man wants you to know but won't tell you is that while he's aware you feel more comfortable with one of your girlfriends in the mix, he wants to have time

alone with you. You need to know that *we* know full well why you've invited one of your girlfriends to join us for a drink or dinner. There's safety in numbers, and having one of your girl-friends there accomplishes a lot: It prevents us from making a move on you too quickly, which would advance things faster than you want. It means that when the drinks or dinner are over, you have an easy escape route—something you and your girlfriend have already planned. It also helps you avoid the awk-ward moment that often occurs during the early-date depar-ture. Not many guys are going to go for a really involved kiss, nor are they going to attempt the embarrassment of rejection in front of the third wheel by asking you back to their place. Though we often might act like it, we are not always clueless, and when it comes to your intentions for third-wheeling we completely know the score.

We have our own male version of the "third wheel," and it's called a "wingman." A wingman is one of our friends who as-sists us in the hunt. He supports us in a variety of ways when we're approaching potential partners. One of his most vital roles is to be willing to sacrifice himself for our cause. So that we might have interaction or alone time with our prospect, the wingman will often engage her female friend regardless of how uninterested he happens to be. In other words, he's willing to take a hit for the team. But there's a big difference between a wingman and a third wheel. A wingman's aim is to facilitate the attraction of potential mates, while a third wheel's aim is often to block that potential union.

Let's dig into this situation a little deeper. We are not trying to date, impress, or accommodate your girlfriends, especially in the beginning of a relationship. We want to get to know *you*.

We want to get to touch *you*. We want to get a chance to laugh at *your* jokes, not your girlfriend's. We want to hear *your* thoughts. This does not mean we don't want to be in the company of your girlfriends or even to get to know them. In fact, most guys will actually be open to meeting them and probably won't mind their hanging out with the two of you. But can't you give us some alone time before pulling us into a group? Starting off by bringing along one or more of your girlfriends immediately gets us thinking: "Damn. Does this mean every time I want to be alone with her I'm going to have to outmaneuver one of her girlfriends?"

Another reason third-wheeling pisses us off is that it makes an assumption about our intentions and/or discipline. It is quite true in these times that if a guy asks you out on a date, it's not because he wants to discuss the existential meanderings of Jean-Paul Sartre and what they mean in today's world. No, at the very least we want some type of physical relationship with you. But that does not mean all of us are out-of-control, testosterone-charged horn dogs who can't go on a date and enjoy your company without running our hands up your shirt. We can have unbelievable discipline, especially when it's someone or something that we really want. But third-wheeling irritates us because it bares the nonverbalized statement that you need to play it safe, because you are unsure of where we might try to take things and how fast.

One more thing: Don't surprise us. It's bad enough to third-wheel us, but the absolute worst thing you can do is to blindside us with it. That's an offense of the highest order. I've heard countless stories from my friends who met a woman at a function and asked her out on a date. Everything is going along fine, with a little texting back and forth before the date and a couple of e-mail exchanges. The guy is feeling good and excited about finally getting a chance to sit down and spend some quality time with this woman. Then he shows up and she's sitting in the lounge with one of her girlfriends, who also has her coat checked and a drink in front of her, and shows no sign that she's going to be leaving now that you've arrived. This is a complete disaster from our perspective, so much so that a lot of men will simply leave after a couple of drinks and never call you again or even return your texts. This situation is a bad omen of things to come, so we make the quick conclusion that it's over before it begins.

> **University of Chicago researchers have found that people are twice as likely to find a date through family and friends than at the local pub.**

There is, however, an appropriate point in a relationship to freely invite one or more of your girlfriends to join in the fun. If we've been dating for some time (a couple of months or more), and enough steam has been generated, it's not a big deal if every so often you ask a friend to come along. Once the relationship has passed a certain point, we would be completely comfortable telling you privately or in front of your girlfriend, "Hey, let's go back to my place." It's also likely at this stage in the relationship that you would agree, thus no risk of embarrassment or humiliation in front of your girlfriend. We'd prefer, of course, *not* to have a third wheel, but a little heads-up at least gives us enough time to get our game plan together for the night, or even invite along one of our guy friends so the numbers and the conversation are at least even.

The Oldest Profession Next to Prostitution: Golddigging

Every woman knows what a golddigger is, and every woman insists she isn't one, even the ones who sit in their drop-top Bimmer, pulling the keys from their Louis Vuitton bag, and pushing the gas pedal in their Jimmy Choos—all courtesy of the fifty-pounds-overweight, balding, twenty-years-older boyfriend who they claim they are only with for love. Do you know those bridges that run from Manhattan to Brooklyn? I have one of them I can sell you, too. **What your man wants you to know but won't tell you is that if he even detects the slightest indication of your golddigging ways, you will never make it past the status of just good sex**. Of course, history is full of rich, intelligent men who have gone all the way to the altar with women they knew from the very start were looking for a payday. These men are quite the exception rather than the rule. They are accustomed to purchasing things they want—luxury homes, friendships, businesses, and gorgeous women. It's how they prefer to live their life. God bless them. But the average man who is working hard every day trying to make it to the next level has absolutely no intention or desire to purchase his way into a woman's bed.

There's nothing wrong with wanting nice things in life. Who doesn't? And most women will push back on the golddigging charge by claiming, "I deserve to be treated like a woman," or, "Wanting nice things doesn't mean I'm only in it for the payout." While an argument can be made in both cases, in a man's mind these are very fine distinctions that he's observing under a microscope and you don't even know it. True, he might be taking you to expensive dinners, treating you to a day at the spa, and buying you a nice handbag on your birthday, but be fully aware that he is keeping track. The sad part for women who want all of this stuff is that they typically have little or no talent when it comes to disguising their materialistic intentions.

One of my best friends has been making a lot of money for a long time, and he has dated some of the most beautiful women in the world. One was a famous model he happened to meet in the green room of a morning television show. My friend recognized her immediately from all the scantily clad beach photographs of her in the popular *Sports Illustrated* annual swimsuit issue. A conversation started, one thing led to the next, and soon phone numbers were exchanged out of earshot of their dual horde of handlers.

He hadn't even gotten into the backseat of his chauffeured car before he hit me on my cell and replayed every tantalizing detail about the model and their conversation. Ironically, he was most excited not by the potential of a romantic tryst with this international beauty, but that she was accomplished in her own right and wouldn't need him financially as had so many other women. The prospect of an independent partner was a complete aphrodisiac. My friend moved quickly—he's no fool—and after a couple of scheduling misses, they finally went out on their first date. It was a total success. They had a great conversation. She was charming and humble and funny. My friend drove her home and discovered that she lived in the penthouse of an expensive apartment building in Gramercy Park, an exclusive neighborhood in Manhattan. She was not only stunning, but she carried herself with confidence and class—a woman who had made it and didn't need a man to provide for her.

The second date was equally successful, and she had invited him up to the apartment that, according to his description,

An international study looked at why men paid for sex. The results:

32% Satisfy immediate sexual urge, entertainment, pleasure.

21% Seek variety, want to select certain physical, racial, and sexual stereotypes.

20% Can't get what they want sexually or emotionally in the current relationship.

15% Convenience, no commitment, no emotional connection.

Source: Men Who Buy Sex, *Eaves 4 Women*, 2009

must've cost a fortune just to decorate. It was their first intimate moment, and on that level she also didn't disappoint. Needless to say, I held on to every detail, which he was more than generous in sharing. But on the third date disaster struck. They were eating at an exclusive restaurant on the Upper West Side, enjoying another quiet meal away from the popping bulbs of the paparazzi. Over the course of the conversation she revealed that her birthday was coming up next week. She would be in Paris for a shoot on the day of her birthday, but the next day she would be flying home and wanted him to pick her up at the airport. Not a problem. My friend immediately started thinking of what he could do creatively to surprise her on her birthday, but there was no need. In her sexy whisper of a voice, she informed him that she wanted a fish tank for her apartment. "Just a fish tank?" my friend had said. "Really?" She reached her hand across the table and rested it on his. "Not just a fish tank from the pet store, sweetie. I want one of those customized eight-foot-high aquariums that run along the wall." My friend never flinched. He smiled and leaned in to kiss her. He took her home, even joined her up in her apartment, and they had a great night of passion. Then, the light having dawned as he thought about the absurdity of her birthday gift request, he walked out of her apartment in the wee hours of the morning and never called her again.

We want to treat you like the queen you are. We don't have problems with your liking and wanting nice things, even if they're going to set us back a little. And while we want you to be honest and ask for the things you want, asking for too much too early can really raise red flags. Golddiggers might have a lot of material possessions, but they are also some of the loneliest people in the world.

THE HANDLE #4

Take out your wallet without skipping a beat. What would you accomplish by saying, "You're not going to pay for me, too?" Of course, if you don't care to have another date with him or getting into an awkward situation doesn't bother you, go ahead and say that, but if you do, just be aware that you are potentially prying the lid off a can of trouble. If you think that his not paying is an indication of a larger issue, you need to come up with a plan for discovering what that issue might be before moving forward with the relationship.

Most guys will pay for the first several dates without hesitation. It's what men expect, so they don't feel put out or imposed upon when they have to lay down the plastic. But if a man doesn't pay for the first couple of dates, something else is going on and you have a legitimate reason to be concerned. It can be difficult to ascertain what that might be with someone you hardly know, but his decision not to pay could be for several reasons. The worst-case scenario is he's a cheapskate, but it could also be that he's financially strapped and can't afford to pay for the entire meal.

You also need to consider that maybe he's testing you. Is testing cool? Sometimes it's not, but other times a man feels like he needs to do a little testing, especially early in a relationship. He might want to see how you react to situations. Will you storm off upset? Will you be forward enough to call him out on it? Will you not care at all and simply pay for your own meal? All of these answers have implications, and he might be trying to provoke a response to get a better handle on who you are. It's always a safe play to be smooth and low-key. If you don't like his not paying for your meal, then simply tell him that the next time he invites you out. It never hurts to have a subsequent conversation about expectations. "So, just to be clear, are we going to always go dutch, or do you prefer to alternate?" Paying your own way in and of itself is not a bad thing, but if you feel uncomfortable doing it or are suspicious of his motives, the sooner you can get that cleared up, the sooner you will feel comfortable about moving forward.

CHEAT SHEET

WHAT YOU KNOW *NOW*

Men want you to need them, but only up to a point.

Proper spacing is not only fundamental to a good offense in basketball, it's fundamental to successful relationships as well.

Men would be extremely appreciative if you helped to relieve the holiday pressure by lowering expectations and mandates.

Men want you to have your spot and they want to have their own.

Men do not want you to have a key to their place early in a relationship.

If you have a roommate, it would make things a lot easier on the relationship if you had your own bedroom that had a heavy door and a lock.

While men are aware you feel more comfortable early on with one of your girlfriends in the mix, they want to have this time to be for just the two of you.

If men detect even the slightest indication of your golddigging ways, you will never make it past the status of just good in bed.

THE
FIFTH

SEX IN THE MORNING

One sign we look for early in the relationship is sex in the morning. Your willingness to have some fun before breakfast and heading off to your morning obligations tells us a lot more about you besides the fact that your libido also rises with the sun. Sex in the morning can be symbolic of the kind of person you really are.

MEN LIKE SEX in the morning. Men like sex in the afternoon. Men like sex in the evening. Simply put, unless physically compromised, there's rarely a moment when a man doesn't like sex. But it's sex in the morning that can set the stage for bigger things. Your willingness to get it done without all the fuss of perfect makeup and styled hair sends strong, positive signals to us that we are extremely happy to receive. Yes, releasing some steam in the morning provides us with physical pleasure, but it actually goes beyond the physical. Being willing to have sex in the morning is a statement about you, and if you're the one who initiates the sex it can make an even stronger statement.

> **28% of men say the time of day they are most likely to be in the mood for sex is in the morning after they wake up. This is only second to "before I go to bed," which came in at 34%.**
>
> Source: menshealth.com

Be Aggressive. Pleeeeeaaaase!

There's always been a controversy about female aggression in a relationship. How much is too much? How much is enough? I have heard many of my female friends endlessly debate the pros and cons of being aggressive, whether it's in pursuit of a man or accelerating a relationship they're already in. **What your man wants you to know but won't tell you is that he doesn't want a wallflower. He wants to be with someone willing to display a reasonable amount of aggression.** It is a widely held belief that men prefer submissive women who don't challenge us but rather sit back and do as we say and accept what we give them. This is so far from the truth it's laughable. Admittedly, submissiveness might've been what was expected of women in the past, but that time has come and gone. Thankfully.

Men want women to be partners in a relationship, not servants. If you're involved with a man who treats you like anything less than a partner, you need to seriously reevaluate your relationship and decide whether it's the right situation for you. Some women, unfortunately, resign themselves to staying in these imbalanced relationships because they erroneously think it's the best they can do. This is a major mistake and will only deliver a continuous stream of disappointment and heartache. I have lived most of my life watching women I love accept less than what they deserved, either because they had low self-esteem or they thought they could change the man in their life. Both assumptions were completely flawed, and as a result they suffered a revolving door of inadequate, good-for-nothing men who took advantage of them and abused them emotionally.

Well, certain men have the same olfactory acuity when it comes to detecting weakness and vulnerability in women. You might think you're putting up a tough, I'm-not-to-be-messed-with façade, but please understand that these men are smarter and more instinctual in this situation than you might give them credit for. They have honed a variety of tests so subtle that, once employed, you have no idea you're even being tested. When the results are in they map out your vulnerabilities with relative ease. Once they have this map, they'll push emotional buttons, leverage your desire to be with them, and convince you that the problems in your relationship are your fault alone.

Partnership is a two-way street, and it means sharing the responsibility for a lot of needs—financial, emotional, creative, and yes, sexual. We want you to be a substantial contributor to the whole relationship, not just part of it. Of course, there will be certain domains within the relationship where one of us will be more proficient and adept, which is completely normal. You might be a successful lawyer at a robust firm and make a considerable salary, while he might be a guidance counselor at a small public high school. Obviously, the amounts of disposable income are going to be severely mismatched, but you both can financially contribute to the relationship, even if it means you will be taking on the lion's share. Many women think that men are embarrassed when they make less money or have a less high-profile job. Some of us are, but most of us are comfortable in our skin and accept the reality that working, for example, as a ranger for the Parks Service—a job we thoroughly enjoy—is not going to deliver the same financial benefits as your job investing money on Wall Street. We are your biggest cheerleaders when it comes to the success of your career, but we still want our relationship to be one of your top priorities, and we expect your behavior to confirm it.

We want you to be aggressive not just in aspects of our relationship, but in getting the most out of life. Men are attracted to women who have ambitions and dreams, not women who just want to go along for the ride. We don't always want to be in charge of picking the restaurant, deciding which movie we're going to see, or where we're going on vacation. Although it's part of our cultural DNA to want to take charge of a situation and make decisions, sometimes we want to sit back and be a passive participant in the decision-making. We want you to take the lead sometimes. It's not about your being bossy, as this definitely won't work, but it's about your taking charge and making things happen. While you might think we enjoy having it our way all of the time, the truth is that we often feel the pressure of making decisions and it is a great relief for us when you take control of the wheel. This is particularly true when it comes to sex.

THE SITUATION

You wake up in the morning to find your man lying on top of you and your shirt halfway up. He's totally into it. When your eyes finally focus, you can see a mischievous smile on his face. He finally gets your T-shirt off and starts kissing you about the neck and working his tongue softly. It feels really good and you can tell that he's *feeling* really good, too.

Your relationship thus far has been very gratifying, except for the sex. There have been a lot of starts and stops and hiccups along the way. Your moods haven't always been in synch and there have been times that he hasn't been able to get it up or maintain it. You know he's been self-conscious about this, but you're certain he doesn't have a medical problem that's affecting his arousal. You're convinced it's completely psychological and will get better over time, so you're supportive and patient and careful not to make a big deal about it because you don't want to make things even worse.

When last night's amorous attempts didn't go very well, he quietly rolled back over to his side of the bed and fell asleep. You felt bad for him, but you let it go so as not to stir up more embarrassment than he was already feeling. Now it's morning and he's in a groove. You know that he not only wants it, but given how things have been, he *needs* it. This will do wonders for his confidence.

Then it happens. You get that sudden, almost uncontrollable urge to tinkle. You try to ignore it, but it won't go away. You try tightening your legs, but it still won't go away. You can feel him on your leg and you know he's just about to go in for the score. You're in a real jam. A quick trip to the bathroom will likely ruin it for him, and who knows if he'll be able to get it back. On the other hand, you're not sure if your bladder is going to hold up. *So now what do you do?*

(See The Handle #5)

Your Sexual Appetite Inspires Us

There are certain indelible truths about a man's appetite for sex. (A) While we're willing to accept less than the amount we want, we still like a lot of it. (B) Most of the time it doesn't cause us any great angst when our sexual desires are met and yours aren't. (C) If you are too shy to initiate sex, we're more than willing to get the ball rolling. It's this last truth, however, that needs a deeper inspection. **What your man wants you to know but won't tell you is that we want you to initiate the sex, at least some of the time, and mean it.**

There's nothing worse for a successful relationship than a woman who never wants to make the first move. Even if you're willing to go along every time we initiate things, that still gets old. Sometimes we want *you* to be the one acting on lustful impulses and snapping off our shirt buttons the minute we walk through the door. We want *you* to want a quickie just minutes before we're supposed to go out and meet friends for dinner. We want *you* to call us up late at night and demand that we get over to your place to participate in some carnal mischievousness. In other words, *you* make the booty call. Initiating the action is a clear sign to us that you're equally into it and not just getting under the covers because you think that's what we want. Yes, you can fool us some of the time, but you can't fool us all of the time. We will eventually figure out if the desire for intimacy is truly shared or simply a lopsided equation where you pitch in every once in a while to keep up a façade of interest.

It's not only about your initiating sex; it's also your timing that can make a big impression. Most men fantasize about waking up in the morning by a partner undertaking her own physical exploration as we groggily come to life. You will be hard pressed to find a man who would prefer the pleasure of another half hour of sleep to the pleasure of waking up nestled in your warmth. Morning sex is some of the best sex there is, and it's even better when *you* initiate it. Some women dread the thought of morning sex, because they haven't had a chance to brush their teeth and are worried about morning breath. It's not about kissing and cuddling and being romantic in the morning. Men just want straight, unabashed, unapologetic sex. You won't lose any style points for jumping right into action.

In a study of 6,000 men and women, 66% of men wished their partner initiated sex more often. Only 35% of women felt the same.

Source: menshealth.com, 2006

I had a friend who was the envy of our group, because he was always telling us stories about how his girl had no qualms about making things happen, even if he were sound asleep and unable to respond in kind. It didn't hurt that he was a masterful storyteller, and we hung on to every word he said, devouring every minute detail and allowing our own imaginations to run wild with the possibility of this happening to us at the crack of dawn. He was very honest in revealing that his morning sessions didn't last as long as the ones at night, and often he was not very skilled or energized to satisfy her, but the quality of his orgasm in the morning rivaled the ones he experienced during longer sessions and sometimes were even better. A large part of his satisfaction he attributed to the simple fact that she was the one who had jumped on him and not vice versa.

Just in case you think that a man's morning drive is nothing more than his oversized libido, think again. There's real science behind why men like it in the morning. From a biological standpoint, research has shown that men have several uncontrolled erections while sleeping as blood circulation increases to the genitalia. A man's testosterone is at its peak in the early morning hours, which is also why our soldier wakes up at attention, ready to go to war. Research has also shown that people who start their day with sexual activity are typically happier throughout the day than those who opted to smack the snooze button for the fourth or fifth time. One reason is that sex releases the feel-good hormone called oxytocin, a magical chemical that makes you feel warm and relaxed. Morning friskiness can also boost levels of the immune system antibody IgA that helps guard against infection. Who knew that morning sex was such great medicine?

What your man wants you to know but won't tell you is that he will do almost anything when you share his appetite for sex. He'll do even more when you sometimes take over the role of firestarter. Why does this matter so much to him? First, regardless of how much he enjoys sex, he doesn't want to feel like he's dragging or bribing you to participate when you really don't want it. Second, sometimes he, too, would like to be pampered and nurtured. Third, a sexually satisfied relationship is often healthier, one that lasts longer and provides greater happiness. Research has consistently shown that couples who are happy in bed together most often are happy overall in their committed relationship.

An Addict Awaits

What your man wants you to know but won't tell you is that receiving good oral sex is sometimes better than intercourse. Men love to receive oral sex, so much so that even if the technique isn't the greatest, it's still enjoyed and can become truly addictive. Don't necessarily be easy, but still be somewhat aggressive when it comes to oral sex. It makes me think of the expression, "The quickest way to a man's heart is through his stomach." Well, maybe that's why there's such an obesity problem. Actually, the quickest way to a man's heart is through his loins. Men will go to the ends of the earth for oral pleasure. And if you're good at it—a skill that will shine brightly on your résumé—he will do a Superman and even leap tall buildings in a single bound.

> **77% of men between the ages of 25–39 have received oral sex from women within the past year. 62% of men from ages 40–49 have received oral sex from women within the past year.**
>
> Source: National Survey of Sexual Health and Behavior, 2010

What greatly pleases your man is not only that you are willing to be generous with your oral skills, but you also show or express that you enjoy seeing the pleasure those skills bring him. I once asked some of my female friends their opinions about pleasuring their men. Their answers were quite insightful, but there was one that stuck with me. "I don't exactly love going down on him, but I know how much he likes it, and I see how vulnerable it makes him. I get turned on not by the act of doing it, but by how intense his pleasure is." That's the kind of attitude that can win a man's heart over a thousand times. The fact that she's doing something that is not on the top of her own satisfaction list but knows it's on the top of her man's is what keeps a partner engaged and wanting to do more for her *and* the relationship.

Sexual relationships are always about give and take. By no means am I saying that the pleasure you give shouldn't be returned to you—reciprocity is critical so both parties feel as though they're getting as good as they're giving. But you must understand the power you hold in your ability to make men feel so good so quickly. Don't throw away that power, but savor it and use it wisely. Believe me, gratitude will flow like a mighty river.

> **Women and men were more likely to experience orgasm during their most recent sexual event if, during that event, they engaged in a greater number of sexual behaviors.**
>
> Source: National Survey of Sexual
> Health and Behavior, 2010

The Power of Yeeeeeeeees!

Initiating doesn't apply only to getting things going in the beginning of a sexual encounter. There are also several key initiation points within the encounter. Deciding when the clothes come off, time of entrance, position changes—there are plenty of opportunities for you to demonstrate some control. But one that is most appreciated and might surprise you? Verbal banter. Just a few words mixed in with the sounds of pleasure can turn a good experience into one that is truly great.

Yes, men don't mind hearing how good they are or how well-endowed our instrument is—this, of course, with the caveat that the praise must ring true. False praise—even if detected only once—can lead to terminal mistrust.

A little talk can make your man go crazy—in a good way. It doesn't have to be a full-on conversation and he damn sure doesn't want to feel like he's driving down the highway listening to an audio book. But just a few comments here and there synchronized with the action can turn a good experience into something sublime. Some women are either very shy about verbal exchanges during sex or simply don't know what to say. Overcoming shyness takes time and patience, and your man understands that, so step a little out of your comfort zone and try it out. Try a little at a time and it becomes an acquired taste.

5 THINGS GUYS WANT YOU TO KNOW

If you're truly interested, don't play too hard to get.

When the bathroom door is closed, please don't stand outside and ask us questions. Unless there's a raging fire, it can wait.

There is rarely a time when we're not up for sex.

Just because we crave physical contact, it doesn't mean we want or expect everything to lead to sex.

Sometimes we want other guys to look at you, so don't be afraid to wear something a *little* tighter and shorter.

But a man's desire to hear your words of joy go much deeper than that. Men have an almost unmatched desire to please their woman and to make sure that the experience is mutually enjoyable. Are some men selfish? Absolutely. Are there times when men only think about their own satisfaction? Absolutely. But most of the time men are searching and working for your pleasure, too.

While "yeeesssss" is the internationally understood proclamation of pleasure, more creativity is greatly appreciated to heighten the excitement of the moment. But don't go overboard, as this is another area where making things complicated can work against you. There are a lot of simple things you can say that make your man wild the second the words leave your lips. *Is this how you like it? Hmm. Right there. So this is what you want?* Sometimes a silent experience is completely sensual and pleasurable, but you should always remember that a few strategically placed words can work like gasoline on a fire.

Doesn't Take a Hero in the Morning

It's completely understood that our energy levels might not be equal in the morning. Some men are morning people and some aren't. Granted. But **what your man wants you to know but won't tell you is that you don't have to go through a bunch of heroics to make him happy in the morning.** The good news is that his pleasure threshold is at its lowest and most reachable first thing in the morning. Sometimes it's so low that just a little dirty, sideways look and incidental contact can almost do the trick. Most women mistakenly think that to please their man, every sexual encounter must be some euphoric odyssey filled with surprises and superhuman physical stunts. Thus, they are less inclined to participate in the morning, because they feel as if they will not be at their best and will be criticized for a lackluster performance. Dead wrong.

Despite what the movies and widespread gender mythology suggest, men are not always looking for a two-hour raucous romp punctuated with multiple orgasms. Sure, if they can score that every once in a while—*great* and they're happy to take it. But a man's expectations and desires are so much less ambitious than that. You know how some say just a pizza, a cold six-pack, and a football game on the big screen can make a man deliriously happy? Well, good news for you—that simplicity extends to bedroom satisfaction in the morning. You don't have to wake your man up swinging from a chandelier butt naked with Lady Gaga piping in from an iPod docking station. It takes just a couple of simple maneuvers and your man's awareness that you're willing to make any kind of effort to make him happy in the morning.

In fact, one of the worst things that you can do in the morning is to complicate things. Asking your man to wait while you light candles, spritz yourself with perfume, or work on getting your hair right is one of the quickest ways to kill the mood. You might want to brush your teeth, but even this delay can disrupt the momentum. Keep some mints or gum on the night table if necessary. The key is to make the experience direct and hassle-free. When you turn it into a production, you raise expectations for both of you, and the last thing he wants in the morning is to feel pressure to get it perfect. The morning allows both of you to be comfortable with not having to be at the top of your game.

And just think how much more enjoyable for both of you when you can relax and not worry about whether everything is going to be overanalyzed and recalled at a later date.

Quickies are absolutely fine in the morning. In fact, they fit as naturally into an early routine as a blueberry muffin and a cup of coffee. Unless you're resting in some shaded villa on a Mexican peninsula where there aren't any real time-of-day restrictions, most of us have things to do in the morning and regardless of how early we get up, there will be a hectic period before we walk out the door. This is why a quickie makes perfect sense. It works well from a timing standpoint, and the natural adrenaline it unleashes is more effective than the stimulating effects of drinking a gallon of coffee with half a cup of sugar. Men are completely accepting and extremely appreciative of a morning quickie before having to charge outside and do battle with the evil forces of the world. Not only will sex in the morning prepare your man mentally and physically, it is a gift that keeps on giving, providing him with something to remember throughout the day when he's crammed on a downtown bus or struggling to stay awake during a lecture from an overbearing boss. Morning sex delivers *all* of the time.

THE HANDLE #5

Your sexual relationship has largely been out of synch and your man has not had the easiest time getting himself ready and staying in the moment. This is surprisingly a great opportunity to help him regain confidence in himself and in the physical promise of your relationship. This is one of those situations where you might have to take a little bit of a hit for the good of the team.

Everyone, of course, has different bladder-holding capabilities so decide if you think you can accomplish morning sex. If you have 75 percent confidence that you can get through it without releasing your bladder, then by all means, tolerate whatever discomfort there might be to help boost your man's confidence and morale. Being selfless and sensitive at this time of day can pay rich dividends.

Limit the amount of foreplay (as this will only prolong the amount of time it takes for you to get to the bathroom). This is one time when speed is in your favor. Also, make sure you try a position that is less likely to put pressure on your bladder. Gravity is not your friend during morning sex. Avoid positions (for example, woman on top) where you are responsible for most of the movement. This is also not the time to be adventurous or try multiple positions. Find one that works and stick with it until the end.

Men are extremely sensitive and sometimes irrational about their ability to perform. It may not be justified, but that doesn't matter. Knowing this, select situations where you may have to make a bit of a sacrifice for the greater good.

CHEAT SHEET

WHAT YOU KNOW *NOW*

Men don't want a wallflower; rather they want someone willing to display a reasonable amount of aggression.

Men want you to initiate the sex at least some of the time and mean it.

Men will do almost anything when you share their appetite for sex.

Receiving good oral sex is sometimes better than intercourse.

You don't have to go through a bunch of heroics to make men happy in the morning. A little goes a long way.

Morning sex delivers *all* of the time.

THE
SIXTH

YOUR BODY IS TRULY *OUR* TEMPLE

This is the most superficial, carnal, pig-headed chapter in this book. But it also might be the most important. Your body is not the only thing that matters to us, but please know that it means the world to us. How you package your assets can make or break a relationship.

MEN WORSHIP WOMEN'S bodies. We never get tired of watching or admiring or fantasizing about female bodies. I've seen old men (well into their eighties, with oxygen tanks hanging on the back of their wheelchairs) sneaking side glances at women striding by. Whether we're single, married, young, or old, we have a biological attraction to the anatomical characteristics that make your body so different from ours. Two men who are complete strangers can be standing in line to buy coffee and if a well-put-together woman walks by, without hesitation they will say something to each other or simply exchange a quiet look of, *Damn, that is nice!* This is simply who men are—physical creatures.

Results Matter but the Effort Still Gets Points

There's nothing worse than a woman who doesn't care about her appearance. Is every woman going to look like Gisele Bündchen or Halle Berry? Absolutely not. And believe me, most men won't hold you to those standards. But we *do* hold you to some basic standards. And you can reach them quite simply by understanding your natural assets. There's little tolerance in our world for not trying because you're not five-foot-ten or because you have a B cup instead of a C cup. **What your man wants you to know but won't tell you is that he does not expect perfection, but he wants you to make an effort to look the best you can.**

Men's admiration of gorgeous movie stars and cover models goes beyond their physical attributes. We also enjoy their attitude and effort. These women work very hard, often to the point of discomfort (can you say Louboutin stilettos?) to present themselves at their best. Even when they aren't at their best, they strategically hide themselves behind oversized dark sunglasses and baseball caps so no one can see their flaws. We love this about them. When you see them, they're always together. Of course, there are times they look better than others, but one thing is certain: When they're going to face the public, they don't just roll out of bed and throw on the first thing they find hanging over the back of a chair. They actually take some time to think about what they're going to wear and how they're going to style their hair. This is all that we ask of you: effort.

There are plenty of women who don't have natural beauty, but who work hard to look the best they can. I can't stop thinking about a scene in the hit TV show *Mad Men* where the office veteran, the uber-sexy character Joan Harris, deliciously played by Christina Hendricks, pulls the shy upstart Peggy Olson (played by Elisabeth Moss) to the side early in her tenure at the advertising firm. With a smile that can melt hearts, she cuts into Peggy not about the quality of her work, but about the lack of quality in her appearance. She advises Peggy that if she plans on making it in the firm, she had better start paying attention to the clothes she wears, the way she styles her hair, and how she carries herself. Needless to say, Peggy gets offended. Then she gets to thinking and decides to make a few changes. In this extremely male-dominated, testosterone-driven office, mousy Peggy Olson quickly becomes the most talked about "girl" in the place. She still was not as attractive or as sensuous as Joan Harris (she never could be), but the men give her a ton of points and attention for trying.

Wrap the Package in Great Paper

Very few women are going to look like they just walked off of a runway, and very few men expect that. What we do expect, however, is that you look like you were at least sitting in the first or second row of a fashion show. For us it's not about brands, especially since the vast majority of us can't tell a Michael Kors dress from a Diane von Furstenberg. In fact, we get a headache just thinking about how you all are able to keep up with fashion do's and don'ts. We might not know *who* you're wearing, but we do know *what* it looks like when you've taken some time to put yourself together. **What your man wants you to know but won't tell you is that he expects you to invest some energy in your appearance, especially when you're going out together.**

Today's woman is particularly lucky compared to her counterparts of yesteryear. Today there are so many new and improved accessories to help you overcome physical shortcomings: colored contact lenses, fashionable mile-high stilettos, push-up bras that add at least a cup size, fabrics that create curves where you don't have any and hide those you don't want, Botox injections that can instantly remove wrinkles. On a scale of 0 to 10, these enhancements can't take a 4 to a 10, but they can certainly help an average-looking woman climb into the 7 to 8 range. Despite what popular media want you to believe, not all men have delusions of bedding a supermodel.

Think about gift-giving and receiving: Line up five equal-sized gift-wrapped packages on a table and don't reveal the contents. Then give someone the opportunity to choose one. Most people will reach for the one that's wrapped in what looks like the finest quality paper. The same can be said for men picking out a woman to date. We can't know what's on the inside before talking to you and spending time with you, so our natural instinct is to choose the woman who is packaged best. Nice hair, well-manicured nails, stylish dress, shoes that aren't scuffed and overrun—we take an assessment of the wrapping and make our initial decision of whether to approach you based on it.

Paying attention to details can make all the difference in the world. The right clothes and grooming can make an average woman ultra-attractive. In the same vein, poor clothing choices and negligent grooming on a pretty woman can make her less attractive. Every office and classroom has a woman who possesses raw knock-out beauty, but completely gets in the way of herself. Her hair is never done beyond clamping in a barrette or bunching it all together in a ponytail. Her fingernails are uneven and unpainted and her face isn't covered with a drop of makeup. Her jeans are too loose and bland and her shirts too blousy and gender-neutral. We spend more time than you might think imagining what would happen if this diamond in the rough were suddenly cleaned and polished and put in a setting that showed off her natural assets.

Please be clear that we're not asking you to go overboard, which some women do to their detriment, and layer yourself in makeup, hairspray, and clothes that are trying too hard. Sometimes the look-at-what-I'm-working-with skirt is greatly appreciated, but too much of an attention-drawing wardrobe can get old, and eventually men tire of other guys fracturing their necks to get a second look at you or throwing out comments that make us want to knock their heads off. It's always best to err on the side of understated dressing, but you still need to make some kind of statement. Treating your appearance as if it's an afterthought is not the way to go, and when you do that, you actually become an afterthought in our minds. If you put even a little effort into your presentation, you are primed to collect significant male dividends.

THE SITUATION

You have never had an ample bosom. In fact, for most of your life you've been quite flat-chested. It bothered you a lot as a teenager, because some of the boys in your class would tease you about the two pimples on your chest. Girls were equally cruel, leaving large bras in your gym locker to get their point across. But by the time you got settled in high school, it was no longer an issue. Thanks to your long legs and well-angled face, you had no problems attracting male attention.

You secretly wondered after college what it would feel like to have larger breasts. You even considered the unthinkable—implants. Only your best friend knew that you went to a plastic surgeon for an exploratory consultation. With state-of-the-art imaging software and a high-definition monitor, the doctor showed you what you would look like with larger breasts. And in your own assessment, you looked pretty damn hot. Still, you decided to leave Mother Nature's work alone. That is, until recently.

You've been dating a guy for almost two years. Things couldn't be going any better. He's thoughtful, smart, funny, and the sex is great. In fact, this is the first time you've allowed yourself to even entertain the thought that he might be "the one." Then one day you're lying on the beach next to him totally immersed in the latest edition of *O: The Oprah Magazine*. He's listening to his iPod and texting a friend on his BlackBerry. Out of the blue he says, "Hon, you look amazing, but I wonder what you would look like with bigger breasts." You're a little taken aback that he's raised this topic, especially since he's never said anything about your breasts before. It certainly has never been a problem in the bedroom, but on more than one occasion he has tried to do things that your breasts simply wouldn't do. He never complained but just kept on without missing a beat. Now this.

"I never really thought about it seriously," you say—a bit of a white lie, but he's caught you off guard and you're not really sure what to say.

"I think it would be awesome," he says. "Nothing outrageous like Pam Anderson or Heidi Montag, but something just right."

You nod your head in tacit approval. "I'd consider it," you say.

"Great," he says. "I was really hoping you'd say that. I've been wanting to suggest this for a long time, but didn't know how you'd take it."

"You really want me to have it done?"

(continued)

"In a heartbeat." He smiles. "And I'm going to pay for everything. It's like we're giving a gift to each other."

You see how much your boyfriend really wants you to have the augmentation. You also now realize that it has been somewhat of an issue for him, otherwise he wouldn't have mentioned it. You really love him and want to be with him for the long haul, but you aren't convinced that you want implants. There still are a lot of aspects about them that make you uncomfortable. He's looking for some kind of answer. *So now what do you do?*

(See The Handle #6)

Au Natural—Au So Better

There's been way too much hype fueling the plastic surgery craze that is currently sweeping the country. Swollen lips that look like they just got battered in a boxing ring, breasts the size of watermelons and just as hard, nose jobs you can barely breathe through—women are doing all sorts of damage to their bodies by thinking it makes them more attractive. Yes, there is a segment of the brotherhood so obsessed with breasts that the bigger they are, the more they want you. But you need to know that these mammary gland worshippers are a very tiny minority. Breasts that look like someone squeezed two softballs under your skin are not only unattractive, but they also make us uncomfortable when we touch them. We would much prefer a smaller cup size that's natural rather than a larger one that comes courtesy of your local plastic surgeon.

What your man wants you to know but won't tell you is that a natural body with flaws is better than an almost perfect body made of plastic. Artificial might be nice to look at in pictures, but it's not great when you're sleeping next to it—unless the lights are always off. I have a female friend I've known since college. She is tall, attractive, always in great shape, and put together nicely. We caught up with each other for a drink recently and the conversation turned to men and dating. Now, this is a woman who never had problems turning heads in a room. I'd seen guys do the most humiliating things just to be noticed by her. And here she was nursing a glass of wine and talking about possibly undergoing breast augmentation. I asked her why she would do something like that when her body was close to perfect. Her response, "The only thing I'm missing is cleavage. That's the first thing any guy looks at."

Your chest might be the first thing that catches our attention, but it isn't the thing that keeps it. In fact, it is the rare man who settles for one body part as the sole magnet for his attraction. Men like packages. Some are more complete than others, but your best chance at attracting us is by arming yourself with several weapons instead of just one. Asset diversification is not just good advice from your financial advisor, but the unspoken relationship strategy for successful women everywhere. Your natural gifts might not be perfect, but with the proper amount of care and attention, they can come across as better than someone's more obvious but unnatural top half.

Men want to cuddle up next to someone who's going to be the same person when they wake up the next morning or five years down the road. Yes, things will start to sag a little and wrinkles will make their presence known, but it's not true that men want their women to never look a day older than twenty-one. We simply want you to take the best possible care of what you have and spend the extra effort it might take for good preservation. Where things start to get a little dicey is when you succumb to the excuse, "There's nothing I can do. It's all part of the aging process," and then you just let everything unravel without any real effort at slowing the deterioration. Does a double standard exist concerning aging men and aging women? Absolutely. We are completely aware of this, and

> **6,000 men and women were asked which body part of the opposite sex turned them on the most. For men, butt came in first at 34.5%, chest second at 23.2%, and face third at 14.1%. The women had different preferences: 19.8% selected face, 14.3% chose a man's chest, and 12.5% chose arms.**
>
> Source: *Men's Health/Cosmo* Survey, 2006

whether it's fair or unfair could be an entire book of its own. The most important thing for you to know·is that *it exists*. Just watch any local television station and make a note of the parade of reporters that flash across your screen. Most of the female reporters are young and all done up in colorful, tight little outfits, while a lot of the men are slightly grizzled, appropriately worn down, and not even pretending to compete for the "best dressed" list. It's definitely a double standard when *you're* not allowed to age gracefully and still be in demand, while *we* are allowed to. It is absolutely your decision if you want to take a philosophical stand and not give in to the societal pressure of keeping up your appearance. But do know that while you're making a personal sacrifice in the name of equality, plenty of your female competitors privately cheer you on but publicly do whatever it takes to garner male approval.

Hit the Gym to Win

Men like women who exercise. It's not that your man wants you to buff up like a professional wrestler or bodybuilder; in fact, too much muscularity is something of a turn-off to most men. But men like a body that's toned and women who care enough about their appearance to put in the work to get in shape. Even if we aren't in shape ourselves—right or wrong—men still want a woman who subscribes to the virtues of physical activity.

Going to the gym can also give you something more in common with your man. While he may not want to actually work out with you in the free weights room, he is definitely proud that his woman is getting into her own groove in a spinning class or on the elliptical. This might sound a bit selfish—and it is—but your working out becomes a badge of honor for us. When men sit around and compare notes—and yes, we do this sometimes—we are happy to point out that you aren't just a slug who sits around and eats all day, watching Nicholas Sparks movies with a box of Kleenex and bowl of popcorn. Just like mothers can't get enough of informing anyone who will listen that their son is in law or medical school, we can't get enough of letting everyone else know that you care enough about what you look like to hit the gym on the regular.

A woman who exercises has a certain attitude about herself that men love. You tend to exude a type of confidence that we find attractive on many levels. I remember seeing an attractive woman with a great figure jogging early one morning in the middle of a light snow. From a physical standpoint she didn't *need* to be out there that morning and could've skipped one run without any detriment to her appearance. But no, while others were up in their apartments fussing over what they could wear that day to look cute in the snow, she was hitting the pavement and sticking to her routine. That makes more of a statement to a man than you'll ever know. Not only does it garner our respect, but it lets us know that you are a woman who can be phenomenally sexy, yet tough when the need arises—an ideal pairing that we place at the top of the priority list when searching for prospective companions.

Avoid the Boyfriend 15

Everyone is familiar with the Freshman 15—those extra pounds that are put on during the first year of college. (The truth is most freshmen don't gain that much weight in a year, but they do gain somewhere between three to five pounds, and contrary to popular belief, men tend to gain more weight than women.) Well, there's something I like to call the "Boyfriend 15." Once the serious dating stage is over and the relationship moves into the formal boyfriend-girlfriend phase, a woman gets comfortable; she has her catch and no longer needs to be at the top of her physical game. So she stops working out as hard and watching what she eats. She thinks she doesn't need to impress anyone because she's no longer on the market and neither are you.

What your man wants you to know but won't tell you is that if you lose your body then you'll lose him. I can already see the eye-rolling and the chorus of "Our relationship is more than just physical! If he loves me for me, then it's not about what I look like, but what's inside of me." This might be your opinion, and it might be romantic, but it isn't realistic. Your man may want to spend time with you because you're funny and smart and can talk about sports all day long, but these aren't the attributes that are going to get him into bed and keep him there. Your body and the way you present it to him (as well as your bedroom talents) are what's going to keep him sexually engaged.

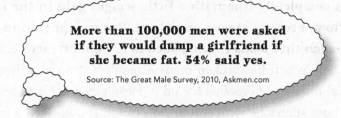

More than 100,000 men were asked if they would dump a girlfriend if she became fat. 54% said yes.

Source: The Great Male Survey, 2010, Askmen.com

Sure, a big reason for infidelity is that some men simply want sexual variety and, regardless of what measures you take to satisfy him, he is simply not going to be monogamous. That has nothing to do with you and certainly isn't your fault. But one of the biggest reasons men cheat is not because they can't keep it behind the zipper, but because they've lost their physical attraction to you. And one of the biggest reasons we lose our attraction? Weight gain. It's already bad enough that a man's short attention span quickly leads to boredom in relationships, which makes it even more imperative that you keep things together physically once you settle down. So don't relax your standards.

The Dreaded Pooch

The little abdominal protrusion that's sticking out over the waistline of your jeans or skirt? Not attractive. No, seriously—it's an instant turn-off. I can't tell you how many times I've heard the story from other men about seeing gorgeous women. They say the same thing. Great hair. Amazing smile. Flawless skin. Then she stands up and the slow-motion fantasy film comes to an abrupt and jarring end, like the film has gotten stuck in the feeder and the frame freezes. The perfect specimen who seconds ago prompted grand visions has . . . *the dreaded pooch*. **What your man wants you to know but won't tell you is that he's completely fine with a little weight gain in the face, bottom, breasts, almost anywhere. But weight gain in the stomach that leads to the pooch is . . . not attractive.**

The pooch has broken many a man's heart and wilted an equal number of erections. And it doesn't even have to be one of those stomachs with actual rolls of fat. It takes just a small bump on an otherwise phenomenal body to be the second fastest way to spoil a good thing. (We'll discuss the fastest way in the next section.) Please don't try fooling yourself. You know that you have a pooch, but you're hoping and praying that no one else will see it. Be assured that we can if you're not wearing the right outfit. Which leads us to the first bit of advice for correcting the problem: *hide it!* That's right. If you have one— even a small one—please do what it takes to keep it hidden. This sounds a little judgmental, but it's the absolute truth, and it can save you a lot of disappointment. A man can't dislike something he can't see.

There are things—short of surgery—you can do to keep a

man's grand illusions intact. At the top of the list—don't wear a tight pair of jeans in conjunction with a tight, thin top made of stretchy material. The tight waistband of your jeans might make you look glorious from behind, but one of the unfortunate side effects is that it will actually squeeze the pooch up so that it's more of a concentrated abdominal mass. Add that thin, stretchy shirt material and we have a really unfortunate situation. Those shirts might be great for your breasts, but they are the absolute worst enemies of your pooch because they show *everything*. The entire fraternity of men wants you to go ahead and wear those tight jeans, but choose a shirt that isn't so tight, and thus not as revealing of that little bump.

Never in our wildest imaginations would we pretend to be experts on women's fashion, but we do know that there are plenty of blouses and sweaters that can do a terrific job of hiding the pooch. This is not to say that you have to wear your boyfriend's double XL NFL jersey just to keep the bump hidden. You can still wear something that meets your fashion standards but at the same time does the trick of leaving our unblemished view of your physical glory intact, such as Spanx body-shapers. Most men don't even know they exist, but they're downright magical for women in need of a little abdominal tuck. This is absolutely not a plea for you to undergo liposuction or any other procedure to remove that stubborn pocket of fat, because dressing creatively can do the same thing for far less money and no assault on your body.

When men talk among themselves about the pooch and how it can take a spectacular prospect and turn her into a head-shaking disappointment, they are not being harsh. We don't expect every woman to have the ripped stomach of Janet Jackson when she's touring for her new album. In fact, you need to know that a too-hard body is also not a good thing. Men want you to be in shape, but we don't want you cut from rock. No man wants to reach out to touch his woman, but then feel like he's caressing another man. Too many taut muscles can appear masculine, and the last thing your man wants is to feel like he's lying down next to someone with a harder body than his.

Everything Was Spectacular Until She Opened Her Mouth

The most underrated physical aspect of a woman is her teeth. The reason it's so underrated is we don't think about someone's mouth unless it happens to exist on either extreme—teeth so perfect they belong on a toothpaste commercial, or so jacked up they belong on a Halloween card. **What your man wants you to know but won't tell you is that he can overcome a lot of physical shortcomings, but overcoming bad teeth is virtually impossible.** A little extra fat on the hips or a bad haircut can be changed, but teeth are always there and can't be changed, regardless of how colorful or glittery the lipstick. Bad teeth can be improved to some extent, but they require a skilled dentist.

Our fascination with teeth is really connected to the power of kissing. While it is generally believed that all we care about is jumping into bed and getting your clothes off, most of us fantasize about what it would be like to passionately kiss a woman we are attracted to. Kissing alone may not bring us to orgasm, but a great kiss is something we all crave and in many instances all we need. There's a saying that a hooker is more likely to have intercourse with her john than kiss them, and that's because kissing is arguably more intimate than the act of sex itself. It's difficult for us to imagine that intimacy if your mouth resembles that of Hannibal Lecter's when he's wearing that wired face mask.

Every guy has a bad grill story. Mine happened many years ago at a really popular nightclub in the Meatpacking District in New York City. My friends and I were having a round of drinks in a booth that had prime viewing area of the dance floor and bar on the other side of it. It was well into the night and the flow of beautiful women was nonstop, living up to every expectation we had of one of the city's hottest night spots. I noticed a group of women at three o'clock. There were four of them and they were all dressed well, and totally done up in the sophisticated, sexy way that Manhattan girls do so well. One of my friends caught the eyes of the most attractive of the group. At first she made it seem like it was incidental contact, but then it became very clear that they both were looking at each other and enjoying it. So what did he do? What any bachelor in the hunt would do. He sent over a round of drinks to her table.

Now, the worst thing a guy can do after buying a woman a drink is to be too fast or too suffocating. So for the next hour my friend went out of his way—despite the strong urges—not to make any eye contact with her, and he didn't go over to her table and introduce himself. Needless to say, it was a nerve-wracking hour as he worried that any guy who had even one eye and half of his brain working would approach her and scoop her up. But experience had taught him that discipline was a must in this game, so he adhered to the rule and distracted himself with a bathroom run and long cruise around the club.

After enough time had passed, he allowed himself to reengage. She was still sitting there laughing with her girlfriends, and while several guys slowly walked by her table, no vulture had soared in to steal his prize. He waited patiently for the right time, and after another fifteen minutes it came. Two of her friends had headed toward the bathroom and the other girl sitting across from her was texting on her phone. The timing of the approach is always important, and any rookie knows there is a higher rate of success and a lower risk of embarrassment when the numbers are reduced. So my friend got up, pretty damn confident that things would go well, as she had not only accepted the drink but hadn't latched on to any other guy over the last hour and was continuing to make eye contact with him. He made his way through a mass of twisted bodies on the dance floor, popped an Altoid in his mouth, and was only feet away from the score when it happened. She turned as he approached. He smiled that you-knew-this-was-coming smile. And she smiled back. *Oh my god!* Her teeth looked like bowling pins after a strike—flying in all directions. He paused for a moment, then he continued the walk.

She was a nice girl, even funny, and her face was even more beautiful up close. He bit the bullet for the next half hour talking to her and her girlfriends, then made a smooth retreat by assuring her that they should talk again before they left. Needless to say, this was not going to be a phone number or e-mail exchange situation. As great as her body was, he simply couldn't extract himself from the crosshairs of her teeth. He even became slightly annoyed at her friends for the simple reason that friends don't let friends walk around with teeth like that. While most guys are not big fans of cosmetic work, this is one instance where we stand in total unison. Do whatever you need to do to get the grill right. It's not like you have to have the most perfect teeth in the world, but they have to at least be in a presentable condition. Teeth should not be a distraction.

THE HANDLE #6

The key here is staying neutral if you're not really sure this is something you want to do. You also have to ascertain how important this is to him. If he's suggesting a possible change because he has a whimsical interest (Oh, wow, wouldn't it be cool?), instead of something really important to him (I am finding myself becoming less attracted to you because of your breast size), then you should not place too much stock in his passing fancy. If he sounds serious and is really pushing for it, then you need to make a careful decision.

If you are seriously on the fence about whether you want something done, you need to communicate your concerns in a way that doesn't outright shut him or the issue down. Convey to him that you would consider having the augmentation, but that there are a lot of issues you need to work through, not least of them a major change to your body that could have long-lasting implications.

The other question you need to ask yourself is, if he wants you to go through this alteration, what is he going to want next? Your eyes, or maybe your lips? What matters most is getting a real sense of whether he's content with who you are as a person or is the physical more important to him. No guy is worth going under the knife for, but if it's something that you really want to do, independent of his desires, then it can be a win-win situation.

CHEAT SHEET

WHAT YOU KNOW *NOW*

Men do not expect perfection, but they want you to put forward your strongest effort to look the best you can.

Men expect you to invest some energy in your appearance, especially when you're going out together.

A natural body with flaws is still better than an almost perfect body made of plastic.

If you lose your body, you increase the odds of losing your man.

Men are completely fine with a little weight gain in most parts of your body, but the pooch can be a turn-off.

Men can overcome a lot of your physical shortcomings, but overcoming bad teeth is virtually impossible.

THE
SEVENTH

KEEP YOUR HAND OFF *OUR* TRIGGERS

Everyone has buttons and both men and women are guilty of pushing each other's. But there are some things that just drive us absolutely crazy. Owning a map to this minefield can help you avoid some hazardous explosions.

OUR TRIGGER BUTTONS are sometimes as wide and easy to hit as a bull's ass. Sometimes, however, we think we're doing the right thing for the sake of the relationship by making them well hidden. That's where we go wrong, because it leads to confusion and unnecessary complications. What you need to know is that possessing knowledge of what sets us off is like holding a golden key. But the key to understanding who we really are hinges on when and how you use that key. Be aware that turning that lock could mean opening up a proverbial Pandora's box rather than a vault of coveted treasures. Our pet peeves are not overly complicated. In fact, like many aspects of our world, they're quite simple and straightforward. Understanding and mastering your way around them will only be to your benefit and produce the results you desire.

I Don't Want Anything So I Called You

There's absolutely nothing wrong with getting a call from you simply because you miss us and want to hear our voice and want to know what's going on. This is completely normal and expected in a relationship. But calling several times a day for no apparent reason is a trigger. Here's what this call sounds like:

SUSAN: Hey, what's up?

CHARLES: Nothing much. Just taking it easy.

SUSAN: Where are you?

CHARLES: At home watching the game. What's up with you?

SUSAN: Nothing much. So what are you thinking about?

CHARLES: Just watching the game.

(Silence.)

SUSAN: Why aren't you saying anything?

CHARLES: Well, I'm trying to watch the game.

SUSAN: Fine. You don't want to talk. I can tell I'm bothering you. I'll let you go.

That is the kind of phone call that annoys the hell out of men. First of all, you don't really have anything to say. Then, when we tell you that we're doing something—a broad hint that now is not a good time to talk—you get an attitude as if *we* did something wrong. What should've been a brief conversation now often goes on for ten minutes while we explain how it's not that we don't want to talk to you right now, rather we just want to watch the game. Then you get sensitive and explain that all you wanted to do was talk, and whenever you want to talk we always seem to be busy doing something else. Now we get pissed, because we've missed some great plays in the game, and we've still not gotten anything accomplished in the conversation.

A more successful conversation, from a man's point of view, could go something like this:

SUSAN: Hey, what's up?

CHARLES: Nothing much. Watching the game.

SUSAN: Cool. I wanted to know if you wanted to hang out tonight. Maybe after you finish watching the game.

CHARLES: Sounds good. The game will be over in an hour.

SUSAN: Okay. I'm going online for a little while. Call me when you want to meet up.

CHARLES: Perfect. Can't wait to see you.

Every call doesn't have to be a revelation of some big discovery or an invitation to hang out. It's okay to call for some relaxed, mindless chatter. **But what your man wants you to know but won't tell you is that when he's in the middle of doing something and you just want to have a "checking in" conversation, just give him a little space and let him finish what he's doing.** This will avoid an unnecessary argument and make us more willing to accept your calls in the future, even when we're doing something, because we'll now know that when we tell you we're in the middle of something, you won't cop an attitude and try to keep us on the phone longer, and that you'll be completely fine with having us call you back later.

Mixed Sex Signals

Sex is very important to us, whether it's just fooling around or going all the way, and it doesn't take much for us to get in the mood. In fact, a stiff wind with a little scent of perfume can do the trick. **What your man wants you to know but won't tell you is that when it comes to sex, play it straight.** The problem is when you give a sexual message—from a subtle hint to pure lust—and your man goes in for the score only to have you pretend that you don't know what has provoked him, or act as if there's been a misunderstanding on his part.

From a man's point of view a sex signal is very simple: If your cleavage is practically smacking us in the face or your skirt is so tight we can see the line of your G-string, it's pretty ridiculous to be surprised when we make a move. This is not to say that you have to dress like a nun in order to keep our hormones in check. But you know the difference between dressing with a touch of sensuality versus dressing like you want to drive us so mad that we can't do anything but try to score.

Every guy has a story to tell about his experience in a relationship of mixed signals. The guy typically didn't know what she expected or would accept on a physical level. She might answer the door in tight little shorts and an equally snug T-shirt and no bra. He makes a move, and she blocks him with her hands or moves away from him. "I don't really want to," she says. "Can't we just hang out and watch TV?" A complete button-pusher. She's allowed him to come over to her place at night. She answers the door with barely anything on. She knows that he's extremely attracted to her. Then she shuts him down the second he acts upon the impulses that she triggered.

Make things easier for both parties: If you're not in the mood, be straight about it. Just tell him that tonight isn't working for you, and it's better to get together tomorrow. He'll go to bed dreaming about the possibilities of tomorrow rather than blaming you for misleading him and crushing his thoughts.

What your man wants you to know but won't tell you is that it's fine for you to set down parameters in the beginning and during a relationship as long as you don't send mixed signals. We have no problem with your setting boundaries. We might not like them, but at least we know what they are. We much prefer this position to one in which we have to analyze what you did or didn't do and what that means to our prospects of getting a real shot with you. Men will respect boundaries, but throwing up barricades at the last minute is *not* the way to go. Transparency and honesty are what is needed.

Overanalyzing

There's no faster way to trigger an instant headache than your knack for taking something quite innocent and simple and getting all Freudian over it. Some women make an art of overanalyzing situations or interpreting what we say. Yes, sometimes there's an underlying meaning to what we're doing or saying, but most of the time there's not. Remember, we try our best to keep things from getting complicated, mostly for our own sake. Here's a typical example:

THE SITUATION

You've been dating a guy for a couple of weeks. Nothing serious, but you like him and he likes you and you get along like you've known him for most of your life. The three or four dates that you've had have gone extremely well, and the last one just a few days ago actually culminated in a little kissing and touching in the foyer of your apartment building. He suggested that maybe you both should go upstairs to your apartment for some privacy, but you declined, explaining that you had to get an early start in the morning. He seemed completely fine with this soft rejection and kissed you even more. You were confident by his body language that he was fine. Both of you knew it was only a matter of time before things went to the next level.

Since then you haven't seen him, but you've talked on the phone several times and exchanged e-mails. This coming weekend you actually have a surprise for him. You're going to invite him over for a home-cooked meal and movie and then let things go from there. You're totally excited about it. One of your colleagues at work asks you if you want to grab a quick drink after work. She's considering a career change and wants your opinion. The two of you turn off your computers, grab your bags, and head down to a restaurant nearby that also has a bar. You picked this place because it's the middle of the week, you know it won't be crowded, and the music won't be so loud that you can't hear each other. Besides hearing her news, you're looking forward to telling her more about this new man in your life and your plans to cook dinner for him this weekend.

The restaurant isn't packed, but it's busy. You find a couple of seats in the middle of the bar and order a round of drinks. Halfway into your colleague's description of her new career opportunity, you excuse yourself to the restroom. Heading back to the bar, you see the guy you've been dating and planning on entertaining with a home-cooked meal and movie this weekend. He's sitting across the room, but he's not sitting alone. Sitting next to him in Parisian bistro style is a gorgeous brunette with her hand resting softly atop his. It doesn't take an FBI profiler to read their body language. This is not a family member or business dinner. They are truly enjoying each other's company. Considering where he's seated and the location of the bar, it would be quite easy for you to get back to your colleague, finish your drink, and leave without his ever noticing you. Then you watch in horror as she rests her head softly on his shoulder, laughing at something he just said. You feel like a complete fool. *So now what do you do?*

(See The Handle #7)

LYNNE: Maria and Clyde are having a little party at their apartment this weekend. Wanna go?

DERREK: When is it?

LYNNE: Saturday night.

DERREK: Mmmm. I'm not sure. Who's gonna be there?

LYNNE: A lot of my friends who you haven't met yet.

DERREK: Sounds like a good time, but I'm gonna pass. But you should still go. Sounds like you'll have fun.

LYNNE: But I really wanted you to go. I want you to meet my friends.

DERREK: I know you do, but my aunt's coming to town on Saturday and I promised her that I'd go to church with her first thing Sunday morning. You know how she is about church. I have to be all alert and focused.

LYNNE: Okay, I get the whole Aunt Sylvia thing, but you can still come by for a little bit. I don't want to go there alone. Everyone's gonna be wondering where you are and why you didn't come.

DERREK: I completely understand, and we'll definitely have another chance to get everyone together. But I don't really want a late Saturday night. I've had a long week.

LYNNE: What are you going to do?

DERREK: I just wanna sit on the couch and veg.

LYNNE: You're just gonna stay home all night Saturday?

DERREK: Yup. Just take it easy.

LYNNE: I know what it is. You don't want to meet my friends.

DERREK: What are you talking about?

LYNNE: Any other time you'd go, but of all the times I really want you to go, you don't want to. And it just so happens that my friends who you've never met are gonna be there.

DERREK: It's not that at all. Not even close. I just want a quiet night. Catch up on some college football.

LYNNE: If my friends weren't there you would've gone.

DERREK: It has nothing to do with your friends.

LYNNE: Of course it does. It has everything to do about you not wanting to meet them. You're afraid you might like them, and then you'd have to see them more.

DERREK: What are you talking about? You're seeing stuff that's not there.

LYNNE: I don't think so. You're very intentional, Derrek. Don't think I didn't notice how you asked me first who was going to be there before you said no. You would've gone if I hadn't told you they were going to be there.

DERREK: You have got to be kidding me. Just because I want to sit on my couch and watch some football, you turn it into me not wanting to meet your friends. Then it's about me being afraid of liking your friends. I never thought wanting to take a Saturday night off could mean so many damn things.

What your man wants you to know but won't tell you is that sometimes it simply is what it is, and your constantly trying to find a deeper meaning than what he presents is an annoyance. When you take things and pick them apart and turn them upside down and suck the air out of them, it creates a problem where there really is none to begin with. Often if you just take us at our word, things are so much easier and less stressful. When in doubt, remember a man's penchant to want simplicity. Whether we're tactful or not, we tend to say what we feel. Don't make things more complicated than they need to be by adding layers. And if you still feel like we're saying one thing and meaning another, or we're trying to hide our true feelings from you because we don't want to hurt you, then simply ask us right up front what's bothering us. This will avoid a long, rancorous verbal volleyball that will only result in one of us slamming a door and hours or days of no talking.

Keep Your Baggage in the Closet

No relationship is perfect, and you should never forget the mistakes you made in the past or the challenges that others have created for you. But just because you remember something unpleasant from the past doesn't mean you can't move beyond it. **What your man wants you to know but won't tell you is that he doesn't really care about your previous boyfriends or the difficulties in your past relationships. He wants to be judged on his own merits and not on the previous transgressions of others.**

A good friend of mine had been dating a complete knockout. He had met her at a professional event full of people in the media business. My friend was tall, handsome, and taking home a nice income, so meeting attractive, well-put-together women was not very difficult for him. But this woman had done something to him that I had never seen. He fell really hard, really fast. Things were cruising along nicely, so much so that he had even hinted at the concept of marriage, which floored us, because he always struck us as the eternal bachelor.

A few months into this whirlwind relationship things suddenly hit a bump—a rather large bump. The woman was having a difficult time overcoming the baggage of her past relationships. One of her previous boyfriends had cheated on her with someone he worked closely with at his office. Understandably, this woman was badly scarred by the incident, especially since she had befriended the female colleague and had even invited her to several functions that her former boyfriend had not even attended. She blamed him for cheating on her, but she also blamed herself for being naïve about his "work relationship" with a woman she thought was only a friend.

My friend has always been popular. People genuinely like to be around him because he's quick-witted and generous to a fault. He has as many female friends as he does guy friends, and while some of them would love to be romantically involved with him, he has done an excellent job of drawing lines, making sure that friends were just friends and not "friends with privileges," and his social life was richly constructed on loyal friendships with both genders.

This new woman in his life, however, simply couldn't get over the fact that he had female friends—attractive female friends—he liked to spend time with but didn't want to take home at night for a romp. Every time he mentioned he was having a drink with someone, she would put him through the tenth degree, wanting to know not just their name, but where they worked, if they were dating someone, and had they ever made sexual advances toward him. Her level of scrutiny was becoming ridiculous. He had to practically produce a biography on any woman he wanted to spend more than five minutes with. He and this woman had conversation after conversation about it, but she simply couldn't accept the fact that he liked to spend time with his female friends, and that there were going to be times when she was invited and other times when she wasn't. Even though everything else was going so smoothly and he had repeatedly explained to her his utter lack of sexual interest in these other women, he simply couldn't move the needle with her and their relationship ended.

> **60% of men and 53% of women agree that women have unrealistic expectations of men and that women expect more from men than men expect from women. Women want men to be successful, share the housework and childcare, and be their best friend.**
>
> Source: *Cosmo* Man Summit, 2010

We are not asking you to completely ignore painful lessons from the past. We only ask that you try to compartmentalize these transgressions and keep them in context as it relates to our relationship with you. Give us a clean slate, not one that already has so much written on it that we have to squeeze in what we'd like to write. It's okay for you to put lines on the page, but don't also fill up the spaces with letters and symbols drawn by someone else.

Digging for Compliments

If you want to really get under your man's skin, start digging around for compliments. It's not only the digging that becomes bothersome, but how you do the digging that really gets his blood boiling. **What your man wants you to know but won't tell you is that fishing around for compliments by saying the opposite of what you believe will only irritate him and make him less likely to honestly applaud you when you really deserve it**. I once had a girlfriend who simply couldn't stop herself from seeking that proverbial pat on the back. A typical exchange went something like this:

> GIRLFRIEND: I can't stand these new jeans.
> ME: Why did you buy them if you didn't like them?
> GIRLFRIEND: I look so fat in them. *(Really? She's five-feet-six and a hundred fifteen pounds.)*
> ME: What are you talking about?
> *(She turns her back to me. What I see is absolute perfection.)*
> GIRLFRIEND: Look at my ass. It's too fat.
> ME: *(I do look and it's really first class.)* Stop being ridiculous. You look great. Are you kidding? Most women would auction off their firstborn to look this good in a pair of jeans.
> GIRLFRIEND: You're just trying to make me feel better.
> ME: No I'm not, for crissake. I'm just being honest. It's impossible for you to look fat.
> GIRLFRIEND: I need to go on a diet.
> ME: *(To myself)* Great. Here we go again.

If it wasn't a compliment about her body, it was a compliment about her hair or something she had cooked. The process of her denigrating something she had or something she had accomplished, knowing full well that the truth was actually the opposite of what she was "worried" about eventually got old. So what did I do? I just started agreeing with her.

> GIRLFRIEND: I can't stand this haircut. I told her not to cut so much off.
> ME: I don't understand why you always let her do

something you don't want. Then you come home upset about it. You pay her, not the other way around.

GIRLFRIEND: I told her how much I wanted off and she still took more.

ME: Aren't you watching her in the mirror? Why didn't you stop her when she had cut off enough?

GIRLFRIEND: You don't understand. It's just not that easy. And now I look horrible. *(She actually looks amazing. And she knows it.)*

ME: I agree, it's an awful haircut. *(I'm tired of going back and forth.)*

GIRLFRIEND: See what I mean? Thanks a lot for your support. I knew you wouldn't like it.

If you simply want a confirmation of something that you already feel, then be direct about it. If you feel great in a pair of jeans, just say you feel like the jeans are working really well for you. If you think you've cooked an amazing pot roast, feel free to go ahead and tell us how much you liked it and how proud you are of it. If it's true, we are more than happy to agree with you. We are not in competition with you and we actually enjoy

5 **ULTIMATUMS YOU SHOULD NEVER MAKE**

"Propose or it's over."
"It's either me or your friends."
"I don't want you to ever contact your ex."
"You have to love me before we have sex."
"We either move in together or call it off."

complimenting you, especially when you deserve it. But when we feel pressured to say something nice or to recognize something you've done on the spot, it takes the fun out of it. And it also makes us feel like we could be anybody: Who cares about *our* opinion if you're just playing a game of self-esteem chess? Eventually we are going to rebel and just simply agree with your self-condemnation. Is that being an asshole? Absolutely. But when we get fed up with your compliment-digging, that's where we go.

An Unwanted Stylist

Some of us care about fashion and some of us can't tell the difference between straight-cut and boot-cut jeans. Some of us like to wear sneakers and jeans and an oversized rugby shirt while others prefer a nice pair of slacks with a black T underneath a V-necked cashmere sweater. We have our own style, and whether or not you agree with it, it's *our* style and we're happy with it, thank you very much. **What your man wants you to know but won't tell you is that *your* desire to always be on the cutting edge of fashion doesn't mean he has to want to look like a *GQ* cover model.**

Let us be who we are. We have spent many years dressing the way we do, and while most of us have no grand delusions of joining any best-dressed lists, we actually have some pride in what we look like, even if in some cases it's not much. The worst thing is when you start treating us like a pet project. All of a sudden you want to change the shoes we wear and even the way we cut our hair. Don't think we don't know what you're doing when you start quietly buying us clothes that *you* like and that *you* think we should be wearing, even though you're aware that they aren't our style.

Most of us probably could use the benefit of a woman's discriminating eye, and a little tweak here and there is something we are likely to accept. But trying to change the absolute core of our style is a huge pain and something that will only meet resistance on our part. Our fault is that we sometimes send mixed messages. Instead of just telling you up-front that we like that sweater you want us to throw away or that pair of favorite old shoes that you want us to retire (like yesterday), we initially follow your fashion dictates. This creates a false situation where you think we are actually open to becoming the dresser that you want us to be, when in reality we are going along just to get you off our backs.

Here's the trick. If we know that you're generally accepting of our style and not trying to reinvent the wheel, we are completely comfortable coming to you to ask about whether colors match, if a particular pattern works for our body, or which lapel looks better on our tuxedo. You can actually have a significant impact on our style decisions—loafers versus lace-ups, pleats versus flat fronts. But it's your approach that will make the biggest difference when it comes to your success in getting style advice across to us. The worst thing you can do is rifle through our closet and start pulling out what needs to be thrown away and what *you* deem acceptable to be kept. Remember, the art of subtle suggestion goes over a lot better than a full-frontal hatchet job.

When men were asked which sentence best describes the way they shop for clothes the two top responses were:

41% I don't look for clothes, but buy what I stumble across that suits me.
28% I buy clothes in big batches once or twice a year.

Source: The Great Male Survey, 2010, Askmen.com

Your Period Is to Blame for EVERYTHING

Let's get one thing clear: Men don't have periods. Now that I've revealed this earth-shattering news, let's proceed. We don't ever want to have a period. And, yes, we actually understand how awful it must be to have your period intrude at the most inopportune times. We *are* sensitive to female biology. We totally get that the cramps and bloating and other stuff is uncomfortable. We also get that that time of the month may predispose you to certain mood swings that are uncharacteristic of you the rest of the time. What we don't get, however, is why everything in the world that doesn't go well somehow can be traced back to your period.

Believe it or not, guys sit around and talk about stuff that you probably don't think we talk about. And your period is one of those unexpected topics that we actually dig into when huddled over a pint. Now, don't get me wrong. It's not like we call one another up and arrange a get-together down at the Golden Horse Bar to talk about the intricacies of your biology while watching a muted *Monday Night Football* game on the big screen. But every once in a while one of our brethren will walk in bruised and dazed, and he'll break into a story about how his girl is being the biggest pain because it's her time of the month. We now know through our shared experiences that not all PMS is created equal, and that your behavior during this most indelicate time can be quite unpredictable and cover a wide spectrum. We also get that some of you simply want to be left alone as you deal with the issue, while others continue on as if nothing is happening. We've collectively learned that some of you don't even want to be looked at, let alone touched. *Please don't. I feel so fat.* While others without missing a beat will simply say, *I think it's best if we use something tonight.* Whatever your fancy is, we are completely fine. **What your man wants you to know but won't tell you is that everything that goes wrong in the universe can't and shouldn't be blamed on *"it's that time of the month."***

We want to be sensitive to what you're going through, but we also need communication. If you're in a bad mood, feel like being left alone, or want some emotional support, we are here for you, but you have to let us know. Trouble protrudes its ugly little head when we are left to our own devices to try and figure out what you're thinking and what you'd like us to do to bring you comfort. When we have no direction from you, we are much more likely to travel down the wrong road and step on hidden mines that will blow up and sometimes create carnage. (Remember, we're men.) What makes the dynamics corrosive to our relationship, however, is when we start feeling like your biology becomes a license for you to scream at us over things that have previously been the norm or snap at us and we can't

Because there is an increase in blood circulation around the genitals during a woman's period, she may experience more powerful orgasms during this time.

Source: Barbara Keesling, *Men in Bed*, 2008

figure out why. It's not like you have to go into every vascular detail about your menstruation pattern, but giving us a little warning about its arrival and what typically happens to you during this time can go a long way in preventing unnecessary fractures in our relationship.

THE HANDLE #7

If you have any thoughts about approaching him, get them out of your mind immediately. The first thing to have clear in your own mind is whether you have agreed on an exclusive relationship. If you haven't set this kind of parameter, you now might consider doing so. If you have agreed on exclusivity, however, then something isn't right. It's still not safe to jump to conclusions and confront him, but take a deep breath, make sure you're seeing what you're seeing, then get your things and tell your friend that you want to leave.

A Hollywood-style confrontation of throwing a drink in someone's face when you think you've caught him in the act of cheating is exactly that—Hollywood. Real life doesn't work that way. There's a lot more involved. A direct approach in this situation is advisable, however, only if you're prepared to deal with an ugly truth—he's seeing someone else. You have to decide what kind of scene you want. Some women want to have that "gotchya" moment where they do an ambush and catch the man stammering and stumbling for an excuse. Others feel as though the embarrassment that it would bring isn't worth it, and things can be handled more discreetly.

If you prefer discretion, leave the restaurant right away, then call him on his cell phone and see if he picks up.

Scenario 1: He picks up. Ask what he's doing in a nonchalant way. "Hey, what are you up to?" If he tells you something completely untrue, such as he's out with some of his friends at a bar or at the grocery store picking up some bread, you have your answer right there. It's over. If he tells you that he's out with an old friend of his and offers that it's a woman, then at least he's on the path to the truth. No need to get into it right then. Tell him to call or come over later and wait until then to have a full discussion.

Scenario 2: He doesn't pick up. Call a second time ten minutes later. If he doesn't pick up the second call, things are not trending in the right direction. See if he calls you later that night, and if he does, then ask about what he was doing earlier in a casual way and see if he tells the truth. Being accusatory is not the way to go as it will make him defensive or push him to cover up the truth.

Remember, things are not always what they appear to be. Keep a cool head. Dignity trumps bad behavior all the time, and if you seek the truth, be prepared to handle what it might bring.

CHEAT SHEET

WHAT YOU KNOW *NOW*

When your man is in the middle of doing something and you just want to have a "checking in" conversation, just give him a little space and let him finish what he's doing.

When it comes to sex, play it straight.

It's completely fine for you to set down parameters in the beginning of and during a relationship as long as you don't send mixed signals.

Sometimes it simply is what it is, and your constantly trying to find a deeper meaning than what your man presents to you is an annoyance.

Men are sensitive to the difficulties of your past relationships, but they want to be judged on their own merits and not by the previous transgressions of others.

Fishing around for compliments by saying the opposite of what you believe will only irritate a man and make him less likely to honestly applaud you for things that really deserve it.

Your desire to always be on the cutting edge of fashion doesn't mean your man has to want to look like a *GQ* cover model.

Everything that goes wrong in the universe can't and shouldn't be blamed on *"It's that time of the month."*

THE
EIGHTH

AVOID THE EMOTIONAL CIRCUS

Unless it's coming from a boxing ring or a big screen, men don't like emotional drama. But this doesn't mean we aren't emotional creatures—we just spend most of our life trying to keep that from you. Get a solid grasp of your own emotions and understand our emotional triggers to prevent relationship hell.

EVERY ARTICLE I'VE read about the topic of men and emotions says something to the effect that "men are not emotional creatures." This isn't all true and it's not all false, either. Do we feel pain other than physical pain? Absolutely. Are we vulnerable to a bruising of our egos? Absolutely. Are we sensitive at times? We might not show it, but absolutely. Are we fearful of heartbreak in romantic relationships? Absolutely. We actually experience some of the same emotions that women do, but the major difference between us is how we express these emotions and react to them. **What your man wants you to know but won't tell you is that he is sensitive about certain things,**

but he's reluctant to express his feelings because he doesn't want to come across as a pile of mush.

Even Soldiers Cry

There's no doubt that we like to be considered tough and resilient. That's baked into our cultural DNA at a very young age. We scrape a knee on the playground and it's bleeding—don't cry, get up, and get back in the game. One of the big kids teases us about our lunch box—don't run and cry to the teacher, stand up to him instead and tell him we don't care what he thinks.

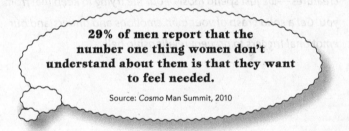

29% of men report that the number one thing women don't understand about them is that they want to feel needed.

Source: *Cosmo* Man Summit, 2010

Someone calls our mother a name—it's time to beat some respect into him. We are forced to be rough-and-tumble and dare not show even the slightest sign of weakness. But the reality is that we hurt just like anyone else, and we cry, too, but we do our best to hold it in or only shed tears when no one is around.

What your man wants you to know but won't tell you is that every once in a while he, too, is overcome by emotions and would like to cry on someone's shoulder without being thought of as less of a man. It's extremely unlikely that he's going to come right out and display his raw emotions, but if you make him feel comfortable enough, he will slowly begin to be more expressive. Contrary to popular belief, ice does not run in our veins.

Cars, Boats, and Sports

It is definitely true that men and women are often emotionally moved by different situations. It doesn't mean men don't have feelings; it simply means that sometimes we get emotional about different things. I was at a cocktail party once with a pretty sophisticated crowd talking to a woman who had been teaching nursery school for more than twenty-five years. Also in the conversation were two mothers who had children in this teacher's class. One mother had a son and the other had a daughter. The teacher was explaining to them some of the differences she has seen consistently between the boys and girls in her twenty-five-year teaching career. What I found most interesting was her take on their emotional development. She started off by saying that even at the ages of three and four, boys and girls were emotionally different. Her experience had also been supported by research:

(A) Boys were not as emotional as girls about relationships with friends. Although boys also formed cliques, they didn't define themselves by the cliques the way the girls did.

(B) Boys got the concept of "team" much earlier—the ideas that you push while I pull, I throw while you catch, you go high while I go low. Boys not only got it but largely enjoyed sharing responsibility to achieve a certain goal. Girls were completely different. It wasn't about team, but about the singularity of their world and how others could fit into it at their discretion.

(C) Boys were far less worried about who they chased on the playground or sat next to them during story time. They were more emotional about the actual event that was taking place. Girls, however, were completely caught up in who invited them to a birthday party and who wasn't invited, whose cubby hole was next to theirs, and who stood next to them in line. Did someone speak more often to them than one of the other girls?

Men are emotional, but about a whole different set of things than you are. It's rare to find a man who doesn't get charged up by at least one of the big three: boats, cars, or sports. We can watch a football game and scream at the television as if the quarterback or referees can hear our instructions or criticism. We can literally come to blows with opposing fans over a verbal insult that's been lobbied against our beloved team or player. Let someone scratch or ding our freshly waxed car, and we can spiral almost into depression. **What your man wants you to know but won't tell you is that his raw emotions can be triggered but not necessarily by the same things that impact you**. This does not mean that the situations we're emotional about or our reactions to them are not justified. In our mind they are, and that's what's important.

Our team has lost a buzzer-beater to a conference arch rival or suffered a defeat that's taken them out of the running for playing in the Super Bowl. The worst thing you can say to us is, "Who cares? It's only a game." Yes, it is a game—technically—but for us it's a lot more than that. It doesn't matter what you think about our team losing or whether you have any interest in who's competing in the championship game, but it matters a lot to us, which means that it should matter to you, even if to a lesser degree. Minimizing or dismissing the importance of where we place our emotions is not only going to drive a wedge in our relationship, but it's going to ignite a retaliatory apathy in us so that when you come to us with something that has disturbed you we will respond by telling you how unimportant the issue that's bothering *you* is. Even if you don't understand the game very well, there is a way to ask questions that show you care that your man is upset. Keep it simple. "How could they possibly lose that game? What went wrong?" You could even try, "Does this mean they have absolutely no shot at the championship?" Answering these questions will let him blow off some steam, which typically calms him down and could shorten his bad mood.

In general, we find it astonishing and even absurd when you start ranting and raving that one of your girlfriends called another friend to break some important news before calling you. In our minds, who cares about the seating arrangement at a dinner table in a restaurant? What does it matter that someone didn't recognize you got a haircut and therefore, didn't give you a compliment? The world is not going to end because someone you know went out and bought the same purse or blouse. These situations can send you into a complex (to us) conversation about who's on whose side and who's going to be the first to pick up the phone to broker a peace agreement. We don't understand why things that are quite trivial to us can send you off the cliff, but we still try to respect your position and listen empathetically as you go on about the injustices you've suffered. We would greatly appreciate it if you indulged us and returned the favor.

THE SITUATION

You're with your friends on a girls' night out having drinks at a popular bar. It's a packed Friday night, and even a couple of local celebrities are in the house. This is the bar in town to see and be seen, and so far there's a lot of both happening.

A group of guys invites you all over to their table. They have bottle service, which lets you know right away that they're ballers. They're all dressed nicely in that metrosexual way, wearing expensive-looking watches and sitting back with extreme confidence. One of them is particularly cute, but one of your girlfriends ends up sitting next to him and they commence to flirt. The guy you end up talking to isn't too bad of a catch, either. He's actually funny, his family is loaded, and you both have an interest in art. In fact, he invites you to an art exhibit opening the next week. But you still can't keep your eyes off the cute one across the table. There's something about him that keeps drawing you in. Is he sneaking long glances at you, or is that just wishful thinking? Your girlfriend, who has had one too many drinks, is practically sitting on his lap.

Your kidneys are letting you know that the second round of drinks is getting the best of them. The bar at this point is packed, but you finally make it to the ladies' room and after standing in line for a stall, you finally get some relief. You freshen up, then head back to the table. You're trying to squeeze yourself between the perpendicular layers of bodies when you feel a tap on your shoulder. It's the cute guy from the table. He pushes in really close and you can feel the firmness of his pecs against your shoulder. He leans down and whispers in your ear. You can't make out what he said because of all the noise, but you smile as if you did. He's even cuter up close and he smells really good. Then he says something that you certainly hear. He asks you for your number. You're taken aback at first, but then you get all excited. The hottest guy in the bar is asking you for your number. You think about your girlfriend and the guy who had been talking to you all night. He's really nice and had already mentioned that he wanted to take you to one of his favorite art galleries. But the guy you really want just asked you for your number. *So now what do you do?*

(See The Handle #8)

The Hysteria of Hysterical

We men know never to use this ten-letter word, and especially avoid it in the middle of an argument. The word "hysterical" is nothing but a lightning rod that has put many relationships on life support. **However, what your man wants you to know but won't tell you is that when you "overreact" to a situation, it makes him forget about the real issue at hand and focus on your hysteria, which he finds maddening**.

If something upsets you, there's no doubt that you have a right to express your discontent. But there's a big difference between expressing your discontent and behaving hysterically. To us, hysteria is unnecessary and a complete waste of time, and the minute you enter that drama zone is the minute we stop hearing what you're really saying and start focusing on your behavior. The expression "making a mountain out of a mole hill" is what we think you're doing when you get into the histrionics of expressing your anger or disappointment. You want us to listen to what has gotten you so upset, but now that you have moved into the arena of melodrama, we are no longer focusing on your problem. We are now thinking, *When is this going to end?* or *How soon can I get out of this conversation?*

Men are not interested in participating in the dramatics. We prefer to package our emotions and even our *expectation* of your emotions in a calm and orderly manner. Yes, many of us men have problems controlling and properly channeling our anger. But often, our overreaction is a decisive action—punching someone, cursing someone, storming off—that has some finality to it. Right or wrong, it's done and we move on. The business of letting things linger for long periods of time or remaining immersed in the emotions of the situation rather than the resolution is often annoying, and our response unfortunately makes us appear cold and insensitive. It's not like that at all. We just want it to be done so that things can move into a more positive phase.

Volumes can be written on whether describing a woman as hysterical is even fair in the first place. In fact, there's a deep history regarding the subject that dates all the way back to the ancient Greeks who created the origin of the word. Hystero- and hyster- are the Greek words for womb or uterus. So a disease of the womb was called hysteria. Famous philosophers such as Plato were quick to associate female complaints with issues that were connected to the uterus. Don't laugh at this, but in Plato's dialogue *Timaeus,* he describes the womb as an animal, a living creature that needs to be pregnant, and if it remains unfruitful (nonpregnant) beyond its proper season, it becomes uncontrollable and travels around, attacking various parts of the body and causing diseases. It was Plato's contemporary, Hippocrates, a distinguished physician and long considered the father of Western medicine, who coined the word "hysteria," ascribing it to the wandering womb in his *Sicknesses of Women*. I know, I know. These descriptions sound as off-the-wall to us as they do to you.

Over many centuries the concept of hysteria has undergone many tweaks and modifications as intellectuals—including Freud—have added their own observations about the hysterical woman. It goes without saying that this term is loaded with all kinds of wrong stereotypes and sexism and is often used in a pejorative manner. But as inappropriate and baseless as the charge may be, the unfortunate reality for women is that it remains pervasive in men's minds (wrongly), so it might benefit you to understand where it comes from and figure out ways to avoid this unfair characterization. Sometimes in life when you're facing a mountain, it's much easier to go around it than to try and move it, even if the mountain is wrong for being in your way.

Men Are Problem-Solvers

There are real differences in how men deal with stress and the emotional responses to it. **What your man wants you to know but won't tell you is that he doesn't like to linger on the problem and all of the emotional stuff that comes with it. He likes to evaluate a problem, figure out a solution, and then move on.** Emotions can be very expensive, both physically and psychologically. In our minds, the less emotional capital we spend on a problem, the better. For us, it's all about efficiency and being able to find closure. That women have a different approach doesn't make either of us right or wrong—just different. Several studies have looked at these differences and found that men prefer a problem-focused approach rather than an emotion-focused approach to stressful situations.

I once had an extremely intelligent girlfriend who had an academic résumé that was beyond impressive. She wasn't just a brainiac, she was also tough-minded and practically impossible to intimidate. She was confident in herself and her abilities and didn't let others bully her because of her gender or size. One time she had spent hours preparing a presentation for one of her senior colleagues. She created the PowerPoint slides for him and explained how everything flowed. It just so happened that this senior colleague had been pressured to make this presentation to the board of the company. While he was a charming and witty guy, he was terribly disorganized and even worse at public speaking.

My girlfriend watched in humiliation as her boss presented *her* PowerPoint and explained *her* analysis. Not only did he have the audacity to use her work, but he presented it as if *he* had created it, never once giving her even the smallest acknowledgment during the meeting. Needless to say, my girlfriend sat there and took the snub quietly with a smile on her face as the board members thanked and congratulated him for a job well done.

By the time I saw her that night, she was distraught. She went on and on about how she couldn't believe that after working several years together that her colleague would pull something like that. She had always found him to be a man of integrity, respectful of their professional relationship, so how could he do something like this to her and not even apologize privately, knowing what he had done? I listened to her for at least a couple of hours, several times thinking that she was going to break down in tears. I tried to explain rationally that this was not the first time that someone higher on the corporate food chain had stolen someone else's work and claimed it as his own. In fact, this practice is quite commonplace in the corporate world where there's a definite hierarchy. I then proceeded to lay out what I thought was a reasonable way she could resolve the situation that involved her bringing up the issue of getting recognized for her work without a confrontation. When I finished my analysis, she looked at me as if I had three heads. I thought that she would be relieved, but she became even more upset.

"What's wrong?" I asked.

"What's wrong?" she said. "That's what you want to say to me right now after all I've been through?"

"What's wrong with what I just said? That's how I think you can fix this with your boss, get the credit you deserve, and feel better about the situation."

"So basically, you're tired of hearing me complain about what happened?"

The truthful answer would've been "Yes!" But instead, I said, "I just want you to feel better so that it's not weighing on your mind."

"Well, what would make me feel better is if you would listen to what I have to say," she said.

I had done that for two hours, but who's counting. "All I'm trying to do is help," I said.

"Well, giving me a solution is not helping me right now," she said. "You always want to get to an answer so things will go away. Well, that doesn't work. I need time to process this, and work through it. Everyone doesn't always want to get to an answer right away like you do."

That was it right there. It wasn't that I had a problem with her emotional response to the situation. I felt the same way. I was upset that her colleague had done this to her, and if I could, I would've confronted him and told him so. But where she and I differed was in how to move forward at that very moment. I found no real purpose or gain in going on for hours about how badly he had wronged her and how surprising it was that he would do this to her. In my mind, what's done is done, so perseverating on it won't make things better. I've always felt that figuring out a solution that will start to bring some closure is the way to prevent a bad situation from getting the best of you. She wanted closure also, but she wanted to postpone it while I wanted it to start right away. Men like to find a solution as quickly as possible and move in that direction. It allows us to better channel our energies and emotional responses. But you should not misinterpret our way of handling

> **Scientists have discovered that men's and women's brains function somewhat differently. Men tend to use only one side of their brain at a time when focusing on a task. Women, however, tend to use both sides of the brain at the same time, which makes them more adept at "multitasking."**
>
> Source: Gender Gap: The Biology of Male-Female Differences, 2001

stress as not caring that you're upset or hurt. We want you to feel better and not allow the offense to continue to eat at you. In our mind, the longer you struggle with the problem, the longer you allow the offender to win. And remember, men are all about winning.

I read it put best by Dr. Louann Brizendine, a professor of clinical psychology at the University of California, San Francisco. She says that while many studies suggest that women are more empathetic than men, this is not entirely true. Men do feel empathy when someone is experiencing stress or telling them a problem, but rather than digging into their own emotions for a solution, the "fix-it" region of their brain quickly takes over. "This hub does a Google search of the entire brain to come up with a solution," Brizendine says. She goes on to suggest that because of the way our brains work, men tend to concentrate more on fixing a problem than showing solidarity of feeling.

Why Men Don't Talk

One of the most common complaints that women have about the men in their lives is "I don't understand why he won't talk to me. He just clams up or leaves." If I was paid a nickel for every time a woman thought or filed this complaint with her girlfriend, I'd be hiring Warren Buffett to clean my floors. Unfortunately, most women don't understand why their man behaves this way, and a misread of the situation can lead to even more problems.

Research has consistently shown that men find it more difficult to express their emotions, and further, that this might not be all bad. Studies have revealed that men sometimes feel the need to protect themselves from their reactions to emotional situations. Men are hardwired to go into action during times of high emotion. Women are hardwired to sit and talk things out. Because men know their own demons they are fully aware that their anger or disappointment or jealousy can lead them to do things in the heat of the moment that they will later regret. Rather than go into that dark space, some men simply clam up or walk away from a situation until they feel able to handle it in a reasonable and nonaggressive manner. Pushing your man to "open up" about things is not always the best choice, as his opening up might mean his acting out, which could lead to unwanted consequences for both of you.

What your man wants you to know but won't tell you is that he is just as vulnerable and affected by the ups and downs of a relationship, but he hides his emotional involvement behind a steely façade. You might be smirking right now, saying, "Yeah, right. I'm the only one with any real emotional investment in this relationship. He could care less." Before you take this position, however, take heed of a great study done in June 2010 by Robin Simon and Anne Barrett and published in the *Journal of Health and Social Behavior*. Entitled "Nonmarital Romantic Relationships in Early Adulthood: Does the Association Differ for Women and Men," young men and women were asked questions about their own emotional states, including a rating of symptoms associated with depression and substance abuse. The researchers' findings were significant: Rocky relationships were associated with equal amounts of depression in men and women, but there were greater problems with substance abuse and dependence among men as a result of relationship woes. Regardless of how tough men may appear, we are not impervious to our emotions. In fact, these findings are in complete contradiction to the long-held belief that women are the more emotionally involved partner in a romance. You might be the more expressive one, but that doesn't necessarily mean you are the one who's more emotionally invested.

In understanding our emotional nature it's useful to think of the four basic human emotions—happiness, sadness, fear, and anger. In the conventional model of masculinity, only anger and happiness are considered to be emotions manly enough for us to express. There's absolutely no doubt that we experience fear and sadness, but these are considered to be the "weak" emotions, so we tend to keep them bottled up and channel our energies into expressing the emotion most available and acceptable—anger.

For most of our life we're taught to keep our feelings in check, so when you ask us what we're feeling or to open up to you, often our silence is not because we're afraid to get emotional in front of you, but we simply don't have the right words

> **According to a survey conducted by Examiner.com, 67% of respondents voted that fathers teaching their sons how to be affectionate and show emotion are the most important lessons they can teach.**

to describe our feelings. Despite the alpha-male image we like to portray, we are very much aware of our deficiencies and difficulties, and emotional expression is a big one. The next time your man clams up or leaves when things start getting emotional, don't be so quick to think he's inconsiderate. The truth might be that he's overwhelmed by your ability to discuss emotional issues while he feels completely inarticulate in these matters, making him feel powerless, angry, and misunderstood. We are willing to emotionally engage, but let us do it at our speed and on our terms. It's in our nature to want to test the water first, but once we discover the temperature won't burn us, we'll be willing to go all in.

THE HANDLE #8

Don't give it to him! No way! It doesn't matter how badly you have the hots for him, this guy is most likely an operator and, even worse, a traitor. That he would ask for your number knowing full well that his friend was trying to talk to you is a major violation of the male code. A guy who is capable of double-crossing a friend to hook up with a stranger is capable of doing a lot worse in a relationship.

The conversation might go something like this:

"Are you being serious?" you say.

"Yes," he says. "Can I have your number?"

"Is it for you or for your friend?"

He leans in a little closer. "It's for me."

"Really? What about your friend? He just invited me to an opening at a gallery."

Now you've reached a critical juncture. His response will set the direction in which you will move. If he dismisses his friend and continues to push for your number, roll your eyes at him and go back and flirt with the art lover. This guy is a complete loser. If he tells you that his friend doesn't mind or knows he was going to ask for your number, then it gets a little more complicated. You'll need to go back to the table and see if the dynamics really are okay among everyone before you agree to give him your number.

In general, it's not a good idea to do a "jump-hook." Translation: You'd be jumping over your girlfriend (who was flirting with this guy) or he would be jumping over his friend (who had just invited you to the art exhibit) to hook up. If you really can't resist the man because he's so outrageously good-looking, then you need to make sure that the other vested parties are on board with the two of you hooking up. If there's any saltiness from the art lover or your girlfriend, it's best to cut the line. Remember, there are always more fish in the sea, and one fish isn't worth losing a friendship over.

CHEAT SHEET

WHAT YOU KNOW *NOW*

Men are sensitive about certain things, but they're reluctant to express their feelings because they don't want to come across as a pile of mush.

Every once in a while men also are overcome by emotions and would like to cry on someone's shoulder without being thought of as less of a man.

A man's raw emotions can be triggered but not necessarily by the same things that impact you.

When you "overreact" to a situation it makes a man forget about the real issue at hand and focus on your "hysteria," which he finds maddening.

Men don't like to linger over problems and all the emotional stuff. Men like to evaluate a problem, figure out a solution, and then move on.

Men are just as vulnerable and affected by the ups and downs of a relationship, but they hide their emotional involvement behind a steely façade.

THE
NINTH

DON'T BELIEVE THE HYPE

It's easy to believe in stereotypes, especially when it comes to men and the difficulties in understanding the way we think. But stereotypes can ruin your relationship portfolio. Open your mind, and you'll immediately collect dividends.

REGARDLESS OF HOW hard all of us try to be fair, impartial, and unbiased, stereotypes are pervasive in society. Many of these stereotypes have been ingrained over years, sometimes in such subtle ways that we are not even aware they exist in our thinking. Because they can also be quite difficult to overcome, I've decided to review just a few of the major points that have been previously made.

All Men Want Is Sex

Do we love sex? Absolutely. Do we think about sex a lot? Absolutely. Will we do a lot of crazy things for sex? Absolutely. But don't come to the conclusion that we only want to tear your clothes off every time we see you. A large libido does not automatically translate into sexual maniacism. I'd have no choice but to shoot myself with my grandfather's .38 Special if I read another article about how men are no-good dogs who want to jump the bones of anyone that moves and has a hint of estrogen. It reminds me of the quote popularly ascribed to a healthy and very much alive Mark Twain: "The reports of my death are greatly exaggerated." The same can be said for the reports of men's single-mindedness when it comes to sex.

I'm fully convinced that our love for sex is misconstrued for two basic reasons. First, sex is a priority for us. Is it sitting alone at the top of the heap? No. But there's no doubt that it remains extremely high on our list of priorities. Depending on our age and station in life, our list admittedly doesn't match up very well with the priorities of women. It's just a simple matter of biology and cultural adaptations. Women typically want to get married earlier, are more likely to arrive at financial maturity faster, and are less prone to public displays of confrontation. These concerns also become important to men, but at different times and for different reasons. The problem is that we don't get credit for caring about them. Everything we do or think gets overshadowed by the prevailing perception that women have about our obsession with sex.

The second reason for this misconception among the sisterhood is that it serves as a perfect excuse to explain all men's shortcomings. We don't want to attend the symphony. *He only cares about sex.* We don't want to cuddle. *He only cares about sex.* We leave our clothes on the floor even after you've asked us a million times to pick up after ourselves. *He only cares about sex.* Anything we do that falls short of your standards has an incredible way of being connected back to our only wanting to have sex.

Save us both a lot of unnecessary hassle and stop believing the hype. No one is denying that sex is vastly important to us, but relegating the decisions we make and the opinions we hold to be mere functions of this legendary sexual appetite is not only unfair but unproductive. We can actually work with a beautiful woman sitting next to us and not want to jump on her. We can be served a pint by a gorgeous bartender and not want to take her home after the bar closes. We can be hit on by some of the hottest women in the room and still go home alone and be faithful to our girlfriends. It irks us to no end when women say or imply that we can't get beyond our sexual drive. Marginalizing us in this way will have the effect you least desire—marginalizing our relationship.

Commitment Scares Us

Give us a break. This business about men being commitment-phobic has been Hollywood gold, but it couldn't be further from the truth in real life. Are we slower to settle into a relationship? Probably. But this is not because we're deathly afraid of having one woman or having to use the word "girlfriend." What mostly scares us is the possibility of making the wrong decision. It might take us a little longer to assess a potential partner and figure out if the chemistry is enough to make for a compatible relationship, but simply because we are slower on the draw than women are doesn't mean we fear commitment.

What men don't like is messy relationships or breakups. When it comes to these aspects of our lives, hassle-free is our middle name. Almost all of us have had at least one relationship ending that didn't go very well. For men, that's already one too many. Whether it's right or wrong, smart or cowardly, when it comes to relationship commitment we tend to operate in reverse by always thinking about what it might look like if things come to an end. We tend to be guided by what playwright and poet William Congreve wrote in his tragic play, *The Mourning Bride* (1697). "Heav'n has no Rage like Love to Hatred turn'd, / Nor Hell a Fury like a Woman scorned." We simply don't want to face this hell, so if we see early signs in you that this might be what we face down the road, we will be extremely reluctant to formalize our relationship.

I vividly remember my first serious relationship in high school. I was madly in love with a girl and through the lenses of my naïve eyes, there was nothing more perfect or satisfying than our two-hour-long phone calls or meeting up late at night in my car when she walked her dog as an excuse to leave the house. It was the classic first head-over-heels-in-love romance. Then one afternoon I was sitting in my grandparents' kitchen grabbing a bite to eat when somehow the conversation turned to my girlfriend and what we were going to do that weekend. My grandfather—forever the sagacious one—said *Why buy the cow when you can have the milk for free?* Of course, I had no idea what he was talking about, but I knew it must've been one of his mature-man lessons because my grandmother shriveled up her face and called him by his last name, something she often did when she was annoyed. Later that afternoon when my grandfather and I were upstairs and out of earshot of my grandmother, I asked him to explain what he had said earlier. He closed the door and sat me on the bed. His explanation went something like this:

Relationships are not always easy. You might like this girl a lot and things might be going perfectly. But nothing is perfect and nothing lasts forever. You can have fun with this girl, but you can do it without all of the hassles and obligations that come with being boyfriend and girlfriend. So if you can go and get as much milk from the cow as you want for free, then why spend your money to buy the cow? Save your money to buy something else and then you will have two things instead of one.

When men were asked if they believed in the institution of marriage, researchers were given these responses.

67%   Yes, I believe it is a necessary institution and one in which I will participate to help preserve.

15%   Yes, I believe in it as an institution, but it is not for me.

15%   No.

Source: The Great Male Survey, 2010, Askmen.com

For many men of my grandfather's generation this rationale made sense, but it is no longer such a popular belief. Yes, there may be times when we want only the good part of being in a relationship and not other stuff that comes with it, but most of us are completely willing to commit. We just don't want to commit to a nightmare roller-coaster ride.

THE SITUATION

You're going out with a really interesting and funny guy, and after several dates that include dinner, movies, and night-clubbing, you finally decide to take him up on his suggestion to go over to his place. Everything has been going well and you've even had some physical intimacy—not all the way but enough to know that you like it and want to go there. You walk into his apartment, which is surprisingly well-furnished, clean, and organized. You exchange a nice kiss—long, but not too long, suggestive of what's in store. You feel very comfortable and even familiar, even though this is your first time in his apartment.

He takes your coat like a gentleman, hangs it up for you, and offers you something to drink. You ask for some water. He heads off to the kitchen and invites you to take a seat on the couch in the living room. His flat-screen TV is turned to the *Charlie Rose Show* on PBS. (Nothing sexier than a man who not only has the looks, but brains.) You hear him opening cabinets in the kitchen just as you're about to stake out your spot on the couch.

And that's when you see it.

It's impossible to miss. In the far corner of the sofa sits a handmade knit pillow that has a big red heart on it. You can tell right away that this wasn't something bought in a store or even the choice of a romantic interior decorator. No, this was definitely a present, and it's not a present from his mother. The heart has an arrow going through it, the kind you made for your boyfriend in grade school. The only thing missing is her initials. You feel really weird getting ready to make out with him next to a "love" pillow from his former flame. You hear him coming down the hall toward you. He's happily humming a song. *So now what do you do?*

(See The Handle #9)

Big Breasts Are Best

Men are turned into helpless lapdogs in the presence of big breasts. That's what your local plastic surgeon may want you to think, but the truth is, not exactly. Do men like looking at big breasts? Absolutely. Do large breasts turn men on? Absolutely. But all bets are off when the stomach is the same size. A man's fascination with mammary magnificence is based in our anatomical differences. Men are attracted for the simple fact that they don't have them. From a young age boys are intrigued when the girl sitting next to them, whom they have largely ignored, suddenly starts having little bumps that push out her shirt where once it was as flat and as uninteresting as his.

Then we're taught by our "experienced" cousins, the older boys in the neighborhood, and the dirty magazines our uncle keeps hidden in the bottom of the bathroom cabinet that Sally is something special because her breasts are large and round and firm. So, just as we're entering puberty and our hormones are wildly racing through our veins, we're hit consciously and subconsciously with the message that bigger is sexier and better. We are bombarded with visual and verbal confirmation that the buxom blonde is the sexual equivalent of the holy grail.

This mammary obsession is largely during adolescence, although plenty of men maintain this fascination into adulthood. However, the vast majority of men simply don't harbor the breast obsession that women think we do. The Pamela Anderson craze was largely a creation of the media. Seriously. At her peak, you couldn't turn on the TV or walk past a magazine stand without seeing her spilling out of a dress with a neckline cut to her navel. Repetition informs preference. You see enough of something cast in a positive light and you also begin to think positively about it. But what the magazine editors never understood was that while some of us found it amusing to look at her cartoonlike breasts with her golden hair extensions nestled softly in the deep valley of her cleavage, most of us would never want our *girlfriends* to look like that. Maybe a woman we're having casual sex with, but certainly not someone we want to take to the company holiday party. First of all, most guys don't like implants. Very few women have good enough jobs that don't look like someone jammed two opacified grapefruits underneath their skin. Second, there's nothing overly attractive about these immovable objects that look like an accidental brush against someone's shoulder or elbow will cause them to pop.

More than 100,000 men were asked which breast size they preferred.

46% C-cup
24% Breast size isn't important to me
16% D-cup or bigger
13% B-cup

Source: The Great Male Survey, 2010,
Askmen.com

A lot of men (definitely not all) enjoy large, natural breasts, but they are not a *must*. What you don't understand is that men would much prefer smaller, natural breasts that aren't pumped with silicon or saline. We are much more likely to be turned on by your other physical attributes (butt and legs) and the way you carry yourself. In fact, breasts that are too big, too exposed, or too fake can actually be a turn-off and make you look cheap—interesting to look at, but that's about it. Don't make the mistake that so many women have made by ruining God's work with man's inferior knockoffs in hopes of drawing more attention. They'll get you more attention for sure, but believe me, it's not the kind that you want.

We All Think We're Spartacus in Bed

From puberty on, men are subconsciously taught that manhood is defined by our sexual performance. It starts out with whether we can get the attention of the most attractive girl in class. The next benchmark is whether we can get a kiss. After reaching "first base," then we are on our way to proving that we are deserving of our XY chromosomes. Movies, television, stories overheard in barbershops—we are constantly bombarded with anecdotes of male sexual prowess, so much so the message gets imprinted in our brains that we are in a continuous competition to show we belong in the men's locker room.

We want to be good in bed largely because if we're not, we think this deficiency will relegate us to the "less than a man" bin. Most of us don't even know what being "great" in bed actually means. How do you judge something like that? Is it how many times you can bring your woman to orgasm? Is it what your woman tells you after the deed is done? Is it your ability to keep attracting more women? Is it how many notches we have on our belt? There is no universal definition of sexual greatness, but we still aspire to wear this title that has ambiguous criteria at best.

We might sit around in a bar and share war stories about our sexual conquests, admittedly many of them inflated for the occasion, but the truth is that most of us grade ourselves as "adequate" in bed. Regardless of what we might tell others, in our own minds we don't delude ourselves into thinking that we are the greatest home-run hitter since Hank Aaron. We know our strengths and our weaknesses, and we are fully aware that others out there have better genetics, skills, or swagger. We want you to tell us that we're good, partly to nurture our egos, but also because we tend to be slightly insecure about whether we are delivering the goods.

I once had a close female friend who had a great body and never had a problem attracting attention. She dated a guy I also knew but not as well as I knew her. He was a popular athlete who many of us believed was strong in the sex game, not because he went around bragging about it, but because he just seemed to have it all—rugged looks, great college, and a hot girlfriend—my close female friend. One night we were having one of our whirlwind conversations about life when all of a sudden she told me that things weren't going well with her boyfriend. I was shocked because they seemed like the perfect couple, and she had never even hinted before that there were problems.

I thought maybe she had caught him cheating or that he wanted to break off the relationship. Wrong. There was a major problem in the bedroom. I braced myself for the revelation. "He's so small," she confided. I diplomatically suggested that men come in all shapes and sizes, and sometimes it wasn't the size that mattered, but how one put his sword to use. To which she responded, "That's the problem. It's not a sword. It's barely a pocket knife. He's so small that most of the time I can't even feel him inside of me." The situation was worse than I expected, and for the next few seconds I worked really hard to get my thoughts together. My first thought was one of sympathy for the guy. I knew that he had to know and how that must hurt like hell, especially since there was nothing he could do about his genetics. I couldn't stop imagining how difficult and embarrassing it must've been for him when after a great seduction the clothes came off and he produced something so negligible.

My friend didn't know what she should do. Intercourse was unsatisfying and she had to pretend that she enjoyed it and pretend she didn't know when he released prematurely and was subsequently faking an orgasm. She wanted to know what I thought she should do. "Talk to him," I said. "If he's that small, then he already knows it. Pretending like it's not an issue is doing no one any good." "But I don't want to hurt his feelings," she cried. "He probably thinks he's wonderful in bed." That's when I told her there was no way he could think that. He might *act* that way, but he had to know—even through the fake orgasms—that he was falling way short. Her belief in the stereotype that all men think they're amazing in bed was holding her back from having an honest and productive conversation that could've relieved the stress that both were feeling but not expressing. They could've addressed the problem a long time ago, reached an understanding, and moved on. A postscript—they had the conversation, he was relieved to have it, and even more relieved that she still loved him and wanted to stay with him.

We Always Want to Be in Control

Society is structured in such a way that a "real man" is the one who brings home the money, protects his family, and makes the major decisions in the household. This traditional profile is largely responsible for a lot of incompatibilities in modern relationships. It's true that most men like taking care of our women and families. This is a good thing. We also like to protect our families. This also is a good thing. But just because we aspire to be in a position to do these things doesn't mean that now and then we don't want you to share the load. And when it comes to us wanting to make all the major decisions in the household just because we are men or make more money—well, there's nothing more Neanderthal and selfish.

Control is a strong word and an even stronger concept when it comes to relationships. Any man worth his salt does not want to be in the company of a woman who constantly accepts his bossing, manipulating, and ridiculing behavior. It's good to have a division of labor in a relationship—you're better at this and I'm better at that, so let's play to our strengths and not to gender-defined expectations. There's a vast difference, however, between that kind of partnership and one in which roles are played based on chromosomal identification. If you have a sneaking suspicion that the man you're interested in dating or marrying believes in gender-based superiority and control, without question you need to whip off those stilettos, turn on a dime, and run away from him as fast as you can. I don't care what he tells you, men who already have control issues are not very likely to change. And if you are the one in a million who can miraculously get him to change, it is going to take some time and great effort. The question is, is he worth putting in all that effort, and what happens if you don't succeed? Are you going to be angry at yourself for wasting so much time and energy on him when you could've been making a better investment elsewhere?

Contrary to the stereotype, men actually *enjoy* not always being in charge and having you take over. While it might seem that the power of being the one in control intoxicates us, the reality is that there is a lot of stress that comes with this "kingpin" mentality. Always being in control means that our neck is always on the line whether things succeed or fail, and regardless of how ego-driven you may think we are, it is the rare man who *always* wants to be chosen for the front line. Sometimes we want to sit back and follow as you lead. We, too, can find relief in not having to think through the pros and cons and ramifications of a difficult decision.

Don't mistake our desire to provide as a desire to control. They are extremely different desires and don't necessarily follow each other. Those of us who want to look after our girlfriends or families but not be "in control" are too often lumped together with the guys who act like they sit on a throne in relationships and everything they say is an edict that must be obeyed. Thankfully, the days of women being subservient and "obedient" are history.

Men Are Afraid of Smart, Successful Women

I've saved this hype for last, and it might be the most irksome of them all. I can understand believing it if you live in a repressed, antiquated, ridiculously conservative society. Unfortunately, there still are some areas of the world where intense female oppression continues to be practiced. But in most of the civilized world men have finally come to their senses and realized that gender alone is not the predictor of one's worth, abilities, or potential. Ignoring the stubborn geezers who can't pull their thinking and attitudes toward women out of the Dark Ages, the vast majority of men have absolutely no fear or prejudice toward smart, successful women. In fact, we admire and respect them, and in some cases are downright jealous of them.

Are women still discriminated against in the world of business? Absolutely. Are women still making less dollar for dollar than men? Absolutely. Are women still drastically underrepresented in the corridors of power? Absolutely. That these inequalities still exist for women is an ugly black eye on all of civilized society, and hopefully there will be a time when these questions will be so outlandish that no one even needs to ask them. But the reality is that these discriminations still exist and put an unnecessary obstacle in the path of women who dream to achieve equality. But it's extremely important to distinguish this type of cultural discrimination from how men as individuals behave in relationships. The two are very different.

I've been around guys from all walks of life in all types of social situations. Never have I heard someone proclaim, "I want a dumb, underachieving girlfriend who has no goals in life." Also, I've never heard someone proclaim, "She's hot as hell, but I wouldn't spend any time with her because she's so damn smart and so successful." Plain and simple, the notion that men don't want or are afraid of bright, ambitious women is simply absurd. Intelligent, successful, attractive people can be intimidating whether they're men or women. Often these people force us to hold a mirror up to ourselves that can result in feeling disappointed, jealous, or inferior. But men who run away from a relationship with someone who has these positive attributes are so insecure you wouldn't want to be with them anyway. Some men simply are unable to acknowledge or live with the truth about their own life, and avoid associations or situations that highlight their deficiencies. Fortunately, they are in the minority, which means there are still plenty of single guys out there who are available and would make far better companions.

Men are more interested in "shared relationships" than you may think. Who wouldn't want a woman who can help pay the rent or mortgage, pick up the dinner tab once in a while, and score great tickets through *her* connections to a basketball or football game? Who wouldn't want a partner who could carry the financial load in the event that something disables him from working or whose career hits a temporary rough patch? Who in the world wouldn't want to be partnered with someone who's ambitious and goal-oriented and capable?

Here's the rub, one that you need to know. Some women who possess these amazing qualities can allow their attributes to dominate their lives—just like men. Men who are so career-driven that they forget about the important things in life—spending quality time with their loved ones, remembering special occasions like birthdays and anniversaries, doing the "small" things—are often criticized, and rightly so. Well, the same goes for career-driven, ambitious women. If you are so attached to work and your drive to achieve that you forget about the needs of the people you love, then you, too, should be criticized. And if men choose not to be with you, it's not because you're smart and successful, rather it's because they don't want to be in competition with your next promotion. We want to celebrate these things with you that add to both of our lives, but we don't want to constantly be on the outside looking in. Intelligence and success and having a great relationship are not mutually exclusive. Both can co-exist quite well, but you need to be mindful of a proper balance so that it doesn't negatively impact your relationship or begin to make you an unattractive partner.

THE HANDLE #9

Get over it. Quickly. You have absolutely no evidence as to where this pillow came from or under what circumstances it was given. There's a good chance that it was given to him by a past girlfriend, but there's also a good chance it wasn't. Making an assumption and getting uncomfortable about it might create a tense situation where there really doesn't have to be one.

If you feel uncomfortable because you think the pillow is a gift from an ex-lover, then quickly move it to a different part of the couch, turn it around so that the heart isn't facing out, or hide it behind the other pillows so that you don't see it. It's unlikely that he'll notice a little rearranging. But even if he does notice, simply add some levity so that it's not an awkward moment. "Pillow from Mommy?" is something you might say that could make both of you laugh. He might catch the hint and chuck the pillow himself and the issue is gone.

Artifacts from past relationships present a tricky situation. You don't want to make too much of them, because they can become more of a distraction than they need to be. If you feel like there are too many reminders of the past lying around, there's nothing wrong with bringing it up in a calm and reasonable manner. What you don't want to do is start making ultimatums. Have confidence in yourself and the relationship you're developing. Men are attracted to women who don't get tripped up with the small stuff and have enough self-assurance not to feel threatened.

CHEAT SHEET

WHAT YOU KNOW *NOW*

Sex is something men value significantly and they are willing to make a lot of bad decisions in their quest for the pleasures that it brings. But there's a lot more to men than some hyper-sexual drive. Believing that men are single-minded and singularly focused will not bode well for your success in securing and growing a relationship.

For men, the "commitment" when it comes to relationships is a gigantic word. Men don't fear commitment, rather they fear entering a commitment with the wrong woman.

The obsession with female breasts that's assigned to men by adult magazines and X-rated movies should not be confused with the reality. Big breasts might be fun to look at, but for the most part a man's interest doesn't go much beyond that, especially when they are implants.

Men are raised from a young age to measure their manhood against their performance in the dark. This virtually inescapable pressure sits on their shoulders like a dead weight, but it doesn't change the fact that most of them know that their talents are far from legendary.

Being in control is overrated, as is the belief that men always want to sit on the throne and rule their feudal court with an iron hand. Men don't always want to be the one saddled with the responsibility of making all of the important decisions and controlling the relationship. It's much easier on their joints to share the load.

There's nothing sexier than a woman who knows her way around the boardroom as well as she does the bedroom. Men will take smart and successful all day long over shallow and unaccomplished. Your intelligence and achievements are magnetic, not Kryptonite.

THE TENTH

LET MEN BE MEN

No man is perfect. Far from it. In fact, we are well aware of our shortcomings and hang-ups. But at the end of the day, we are who we are, and it's a big mistake and waste of energy if you think that you can transform us into the person you want us to be. A leopard may grow old, but his spots never change.

I REMEMBER ALMOST as if it were yesterday my aunt and grandmother sitting at the table one morning, cigarettes burning in the ashtray and steam rising from their cracked coffee mugs. I was playing with something, not paying much attention until they started talking about a neighbor's husband who I was very fond of. He was always nice to me and willing to teach me things, like how to hit a baseball or shoot a marble. I only started eavesdropping halfway into their conversation, but the gist was that this man's wife was upset because he had come home late without calling her. She supposedly waited up all night for him to come home, and when he did, she took a laundry basket full of his clothes, threw them down the stairs at him, and told him he could stay out all night for all she cared. The next time he did that, she warned, she was going to have the locks changed in the middle of the night and make sure he couldn't get back into the house.

My grandmother and aunt sipped their coffee slowly and took an occasional drag on their cigarettes as they exchanged their philosophies on men and what a woman should do when he upsets her. I didn't understand most of what they were saying, but I do remember my grandmother saying something that has never left me. "Sometimes you just have to let a man be a man."

Shopping—Really?

Okay, so there actually are a few men who are clotheshorses. But please note that the vast majority of us are not. **What your man wants you to know but won't tell you is that shopping just isn't his thing and going with you on your excursions sometimes is tantamount to torture.** There are a gazillion other things we'd rather be doing than walking through the crowded aisles of a store where women are giving one another the evil eye as they elbow one another and race to snatch up clothes as if it were the latest Olympic sport.

Before you jump up and start screaming that we don't want you to go shopping because you spend too much money, please know it's not even about that. Yes, some of you spend way too much on clothes that are going to be out of fashion in ten months, but we, too, can be guilty of frivolous spending, whether it's on our cars or the newest electronic gadgets. Our criticism has less to do with the amount of money you spend and a lot more to do with the simple fact that we don't want to be there. If you want to go with a girlfriend and shop till you drop, all the more power to you. But why try to drag us to Macy's when first of all, you know we don't want to go, and second, we'd rather be home playing X-box or watching the World Cup?

One of my grandfather's favorite sayings is, "A leopard doesn't change its spots." That wisdom couldn't be no more appropriate for the subject of shopping. Regardless of how fun you try to make it or the rationale you try to use to convince us to participate, persuading us to brave an endless shopping spree is like trying to talk us into getting the male version of a bikini wax. It's simply not going to happen, so just let it go.

Color Coordinating Just Ain't Our Thing

"Do you like this color of napkins with these plates?" We just want to let out the loudest, most gut-wrenching primordial scream when we're asked something like this. On behalf of the brotherhood throughout the universe, let me let you in on a little secret. We don't give one iota about colors unless you're talking about a car, a pair of sneakers, or baseball caps. It's that simple. Trying to elicit our opinion about the color of house furnishings, a blouse matching a skirt, or a shoe-handbag combination is like trying to pull a bone from a dog's clenched jaw. It's not going to happen without a fight. **What your man wants you to know but won't tell you is that he has very little interest in arts and crafts and interior decorating.** We are much more interested in the big picture and not the small details that make it up.

This is typically how a color-coordinating battle goes down: A couple is at home. He's watching TV, while she's on the Internet.

WOMAN: I want to get some pillows for the couch.

MAN: Great.

WOMAN: I was thinking about getting these orange ones with a splash of green.

MAN: *(Still watching TV.)* Sounds great.

WOMAN: How do you even know? You haven't even seen them.

MAN: I don't need to look at them. I can picture what they look like. They sound good to me.

WOMAN: Come and look at these, puhleeeeze.

MAN: *(Rolls his eyes before standing up from the couch and joining her at the computer.)*

WOMAN: Aren't these nice?

MAN: Sure.

WOMAN: *(Changes the color swatches on the screen. Now they are blue pillows with orange accents.)* What about these?

MAN: *(Sneaking a look at the show he's missing.)* Those look great.

WOMAN: But they don't go with the curtains.

MAN: Okay, then get the ones that go with the curtains.

WOMAN: But I like the blue ones better.

MAN: Okay, then get whichever ones work for you.

WOMAN: Geez. Can't you at least act like you care?

And that's exactly the point. We don't care. The fact that you care is completely fine with us and, in fact, we're happy that

5 THINGS A GUY NEVER WANTS TO HEAR

"Sex isn't that important to me. I could do without it."
"I never want to have kids."
"My ex would do it this way."
"Be a man."
"Notice anything different?"

you care since that means you can handle all of those matching issues while we focus on other things that mean more to us. And let's be honest, you really don't want our opinion when it comes to fashion and color coordination. It's sort of like asking a malpractice attorney what he thinks of doctors. It might be fun to ask, but you certainly don't want to hear the answer— especially if you're sensitive to four-letter words.

Our Grope Doesn't Make Us a Dope

Men like to touch women. And it doesn't have to be in the privacy of our dark bedroom. Getting you alone where we can have our way with you is great and all, but we also like to touch you at times that might otherwise be considered inappropriate or too conspicuous. No, this does not mean that we're looking for approval to run our hand up your shirt in the middle of a church service or stick our tongues down your throats at your company holiday party. What it means, however, is that there are other less sacred places and times where our hands might want to do a little wandering. **What your man wants you to know but won't tell you is that sometimes he is so overcome with his physical attraction to you that he just wants to reach out and touch you in a sexual way and he doesn't care who sees it or what they think.** We have an amazing ability to dispense with protocol and make all else around us fade to black as we live completely and singularly in the moment.

Let's say we're standing in a long line at the grocery store. Everyone is busy looking at the cashier trying to figure out what's holding things up or mindlessly thumbing through one of the glossy tabloids in the rack next to the register. I can't explain why, but it just happens that we get the urge to give you a little squeeze. Completely nonchalant. When we're done, and it's only a couple of seconds at most, we remove our hands and act as if nothing has happened. For the record, this is not about being romantic, so please don't judge us against that standard. We are well aware that this isn't the soft shoulder rub or lightly rubbing of the backs of your fingers as we look lovingly and deeply into your eyes. This is meant to be exactly what it is—a physical manifestation of the libidinous thoughts bouncing around in our heads.

It's your reaction to our touching that is so critical. The absolute worst thing you can do when we sneak in a little touch is to back up and shriek in disgust or horror or cut us the evil eye. Simply offering us a crooked little mischievous smile is enough to make us feel good and send our imaginations shooting off like bottle rockets. You just have no idea how that little nonverbal exchange can make us feel so damn good and special and in the moment, and look forward to the something more extensive that might happen later.

Unfortunately, many of you misinterpret our playful

touches as signs that we only think about sex and only look at you as a sexual object. Yes, we think about sex a lot, especially with you, and sometimes we think about you as this great source of lustful, passionate, carnal pleasure—in less eloquent terms—a sex object. But this is *not* the only way we think about you. These lascivious thoughts, however, should not draw your ire, for they are part of the full spectrum of feelings that a man should have for his woman. If you always want prim and proper and appropriate timing, then you're definitely in search of a guy very different than what most would consider to be normal. And this doesn't mean that the rest of us that engage in this impulsive display of affection are boorish and ill-mannered. It simply means that we are extremely attracted to you and there are times when we are looking at you and thinking how lucky we are to have you. Sometimes we can't or don't want to stop ourselves from confirming that our good fortune of being your partner is a reality and not just a dream.

THE SITUATION

You're about five months into a relationship with an awesome guy. He's not perfect, but you get each other, he makes you happy, and he's independent. The whole love thing has happened, but you've learned from past relationships about the importance of timing, so for now you're keeping it to yourself. You are well aware of how much of a good catch he is, especially in these times when it seems harder than ever to find a man that is attractive, has his head on straight, has a real future, and isn't having five cyber romances going on at once. More important, you trust him.

The two of you are grabbing a bite after watching a pretty decent flick. Summer is almost here, and the weather, after a

(continued)

tough winter, is making everything seem good again. You're talking about plans over the next few months, and he tells you that he's going away with his friends. No big deal. But then he tells you that they're going to Rio for a week. Now it's a little bigger deal, but not much. You already know about the Brazilian beaches and half-naked women and parties till the sun comes up. He senses a little apprehension on your face and explains that every year a group of five or six of his friends takes what they call "the guys' trip." They've been all over—Bali, Greece, Argentina. And you know the guys he's talking about. Most of them have girlfriends and all of them have real jobs and responsibilities.

A couple of weeks later you're IMing one of your girlfriends and she mentions that a friend of a friend is going to Rio over the summer. You ask her who the friend of a friend is and it turns out to be one of your guy's friends. So you say that your boyfriend is going on that trip. That's his group of guys. Your friend doesn't IM you back for a couple of minutes, and the next thing you get is a message: *Check this out.* There's an active link underneath these words. So you click on the link. Then you see it. Sitting on your screen in full color is a photo taken before you met your boyfriend. He and his friends are on a white sand beach kneeling over a line of curvy bikini-clad women, licking shots off of their stomachs. The caption under the photo: The Guys' Trip to Saint-Tropez. *So now what do you do?*

(See The Handle #10)

Hangin' With Our Guys Means a Lot to Us

Guys like to hang out with other guys. It's not about wanting to secretly watch porn flicks together or inviting strippers over for cheap thrills. Guys understand other guys and we like similar things. We aren't 100 percent compatible, but there's always enough common ground where we can even meet up with strangers and still have a good time. I've had this happen a thousand times—whether it's on the golf course where the starter lets a guy join my threesome of friends to form a foursome, or at a bachelor party where I've met friends of friends for the first time. This might sound overly simple, but it's true. Most guys talk the same language and understand the same innuendoes. We understand the "guy experience," whether it's talking about what it feels like to drive a fast car or what a pain in the ass drunk fans can be at a football game. Our common ground covers thousands of acres, and sometimes we like to jump into an all-terrain vehicle with our shades on and kick up some dust in our wake.

A further testament of the natural affinity guys have for one another is that I've seen guys from the cradle of privilege— prep school, Ivy League college—mix with guys who grew up watching their old man toss trash for a living. Our bank accounts might vary widely, but this doesn't take anything away from our shared experiences—learning the purpose of our manly body part, hopelessly trying to please our old man, having a crush on a woman we're not supposed to have a crush on. We have a natural knack for finding that shared space in our universes and focusing on what connects us rather than the things that divide us.

I've had girlfriends in the past who simply couldn't get beyond the fact that sometimes I just wanted to be with my guys. In fact, there were several times when it led to arguments, because she assumed my desire to hang with them either meant I liked her less or there was something devious going on that I wasn't willing to admit. It simply wasn't that complicated. **What**

your man wants you to know but won't tell you is that as much as he likes you, he needs his guy time, and he needs you not to give him a bunch of hassle for it.

I've learned from many of my female friends why "guy time" is such a foreign experience for women. One important difference in our social life is that women have issues with other women. Seriously. I've witnessed it a million times. Competition seems to naturally occur when women get together. Whose hair is done the nicest, who has the nicest manicure, who's carrying the latest "it" bag—the comparisons and competition are simply endless. Of course, guys are competitive also, but not to the point of distraction or argument. We don't care if a guy is wearing a pair of Bruno Magli or Aldo shoes. It matters to us not in the least if another guy pulls out a Louis Vuitton wallet or a scarred lump of leather. Whether he's sporting a goatee or pencil-thin mustache does little to influence our opinion of him, but whether he roots for LeBron James or Kobe Bryant can make all the difference in the world.

It has been the greatest mystery to us that women find it difficult most of the time to get along, especially when there's a group involved. It seems like such a colossal waste of time to spend so much of it sizing each other up, throwing little verbal jabs, smiling in each other's faces, then going home and getting on the phone and talking about each other. We simply can't relate to this, and for the most part it bugs us to have to sit there and listen to you go on and on about one of your supposed girlfriends who by your account does nothing but annoy the hell out of you. Yet you continue to socialize with her, then spend countless hours complaining about all the reasons why you don't like her.

We completely respect the fact that you might not enjoy getting together frequently with a group of other women, but please don't allow your unpleasant experiences to color your judgment about our desire to hang with our guys. This is something we enjoy, and even better, it's the break we sometimes need. In fact, letting us have our break without giving us a bunch of grief works out well for you also. We come home a lot happier, more relaxed, and more willing to focus our attention on you and your needs.

Let Us Look—We Don't Have to Touch

Men like to look at women. It's virtually impossible to avoid a glance at attractive women. This is simply a biological fact of who we are. Married men, single men, old geezer grandfathers— it doesn't matter. Testosterone is the fuel that drives a man's libido. And it should be no surprise that men have as much as six times the amount coursing through our veins compared to women. In fact, often testosterone takes over even when we don't realize it. Some genius researchers thankfully have found the scientific basis for our inability to refuse a glance. They've found that testosterone impairs the impulse-control region of our brain. Straight talk—men simply have a natural inclination to take a second look at a woman and see how she measures up.

There's a big difference, however, between staring at a woman and checking her out. If a man is standing there with his mouth open and craning his neck at all angles to keep his line of sight directed at his target, then that's more than innocently checking out a woman. If your man does this in front of you, by all means you have every right to be upset and feel disrespected. In fact, he deserves an old-fashioned backhand and he knows it. But if your man simply takes a quick look, doesn't say anything, and doesn't make any overtures toward the other woman, what harm is done? Really. **What your man wants you to know but won't tell you is that checking out another woman is not a judgment or statement about you or his feelings toward you. They are completely unrelated.**

There are really two ways to play this: If it makes you feel better for your man to be fake, that can be easily accomplished. Say you're walking hand-in-hand and a woman in a tight skirt with a great figure walks by. First of all, let's be honest; you'll probably notice her just as much as he does. Whether you harbor admiration or envy doesn't matter. You see what he's seeing. So he can pretend not to see her, but you know he sees her and he knows you see her. If pretending she's invisible is what makes you feel better, fine. A fleeting look isn't worth his being forced to sleep on the couch later that night. The other way this can be played is he takes a look—not a prolonged look—that allows him to recognize the exceptional quality of this woman, which he can do and keep right on moving. Even better, you might be honest and say something like, "Not bad." Acknowledging what he's thinking without getting all bent out of shape about it is one of the biggest turn-ons there is for a guy. It shows your honesty and confidence in yourself and your relationship.

Think about it for a moment. Your man is with you not because someone has a gun to his head, but because he *wants* to be with *you*. That woman walking by is a complete stranger. It's not like he's going to let go of your hand, then run after her and ask for her number while you stand there waiting. He's not saying that she has better assets than yours, or that he wants her next to him at night rather than you. He's simply looking at a woman who deserves to be looked at and nothing more. Oh, and by the way, it's not like if he wasn't with you that he wouldn't look. If he was alone or with a couple of his guys, you can be certain he would take a second look of admiration. So looking at her in front of you is doing nothing more than what he'd do if you were not there. Why would you want him to pretend to behave in a way that is not natural or realistic?

On the flip side, if your man is snapping his neck every few feet looking at other women, that's definitely a problem. If he's doing that in your presence, I dare to think what he's doing when you're not around. But an occasional look is absolutely nothing to get cross-eyed about. A look is only a look. Don't make it anything more than that.

We'll Settle for Drama on Broadway, but Not Starring Your Girlfriends

Men don't like drama. Whatever the root causes, we have a natural allergy to theater—not the stages on Broadway—but the stages on which you and your girlfriends alternate starring roles. **What your man wants you to know but won't tell you is that he doesn't mind when you do your thing with your girls, but don't bring the drama home to him**.

Men typically prefer a speedy resolution and not a bunch of lingering. We overwhelmingly prefer a direct approach rather than one that makes a long, wide arc when a straight line would've been so much easier and faster. Let's get the beef on the table, then get rid of it and move on.

This might sound a bit cliché, but men really do frame most things within the structure of sporting events, specifically how the game is broken up into discrete segments (quarters, halves, periods, rounds) and everything is run against the all-powerful clock. Watch a boxing match where two fighters literally attempt to bash each other's brains out over the course of several rounds. Then, as long as someone isn't carried from the ring unconscious, once the clock expires and the final bell rings, the two bloodied, stumbling fighters find each other somewhere near the center of the ring and hug each other in a congratulatory truce. Watch a professional football game where guys are trying to practically dismember their opponents, but after the final whistle, they collect in the middle of the field, the opposing coaches shaking hands and the players hugging one another, even kneeling and saying a prayer together.

We men like to know that there's a natural endpoint to confrontation and disagreements. Once the final bell has sounded and the referee throws his hands in the air, for us, it's over. Whatever happened on the field we like to leave it there, get showered, then meet up for drinks afterward. In our overly simplistic view, the only thing that comes close to our willingness to prolong turmoil is what we see in a good old-fashioned rivalry. Whether it's the Yankees and the Red Sox, Celtics and Lakers, or Chicago Bears and Green Bay Packers, these love-to-hate-'em opponents carry on the tradition of "bad blood," but at the end of the day it's really part of the good-natured camaraderie that comes with the competition we enjoy so much.

This is why our fights and rivalries are different than yours. We can throw everything in a box and wrap it up when it's all done and move on, but you tend to keep it going, trying to win over mutual friends so that they take your side, then engage in long-form warfare where the controversy or otherwise trivial disagreement stretches on for days and even weeks. We're not advocating that you have to always get along with your friends or not spend a reasonable amount of time feeling bad about an altercation or perceived slight, but in the spirit of being honest, we really would prefer to hear it once, work on a resolution with you, then move on.

We are reluctant to wade into the fiery waters of your girl-friend battles because it seems like more times than not we get burned. If we say the wrong thing or express the "wrong" opinion about the situation, then we are suddenly in an argument and it becomes one big mess—a mess we never wanted to be part of in the first place but got dragged into against our desire and better judgment. Please remember that we are ultimately on your side and want to support you in whatever difficulties you're having, but when it comes to your girlfriends, we know that there are a lot of nuances to your relationships that we may never understand. So if you don't mind, we'll just roam up and down the sidelines cheering you on, then when it's all over, take you home and love you unconditionally.

THE HANDLE #10

The first thing to remember is that this shot was taken before your relationship began. The second thing you need to remember is that guys will always be guys. Should you be a little concerned? Absolutely. Should you imagine there will be some flirting on the trip to Rio? Absolutely. Should you go crazy and tell him that he can't go? Absolutely not!

There's nothing wrong with innocent flirting. Strangers talking to each other or buying each other drinks, and even a little dancing is harmless if it stops there. Flirting with someone doesn't mean it's automatically going to lead to sex. This is where the trust comes in. If you trust your man and have an honest and open relationship, you should take the first step and bring this up to him. It's very unlikely that he will, because either he doesn't know how to explain it to you or he's worried that regardless of what he says, you will only think that he's going to cheat on you.

Don't be bashful. Let him know that you saw a photo from a previous guy's trip, and tell him how you came across the photo so he doesn't think you were snooping. Your next step is the most courageous one; that will put your trust to the test. Tell him that you aren't overly thrilled that they will be flirting and dancing and buying drinks, but you're willing to go along with it if there's a line that doesn't get crossed. Be clear and explicit. Don't leave it open to interpretation. Tell him specifically what will and what won't work for you.

The bottom line is that someone can make all kinds of promises to your face, then do completely the opposite behind your back. That's the way many people are, unfortunately. Plenty of guys go on trips with friends and don't go for the explicit purpose of boozing all night and hooking up with random women. If you trust your man and you've nurtured a good relationship, then this conversation can be done in a civil and non-angst-provoking fashion, as long as you both understand each other and are comfortable with the outcome.

CHEAT SHEET

WHAT YOU KNOW *NOW*

In most cases shopping just isn't your man's thing and going with you on a shopping excursion is tantamount to torture.

Your man has little interest in arts and crafts and interior decorating.

Sometimes your man is so overcome with his physical attraction to you that he just wants to reach out and touch you in a sexual way, and he doesn't care who sees it or what they think.

As much as he likes you, he needs his guy time, and he needs you not to give him a bunch of flak for it.

Checking out another woman is not a judgment or statement about you or your man's feelings toward you. It is completely unrelated.

He doesn't mind it when you do your thing with your girls, but he'd greatly appreciate it if you didn't bring the drama home to him.